CULTURAL HERITAGE OF PABBAR VALLEY

CULTURAL HERITAGE OF PABBAR VALLEY

DR. HARI CHAUHAN

AGAM

AGAM KALA PRAKASHAN
DELHI

First Published 2012

ISBN : 978-81-7320-123-3

Published by:
Dr. Agam Prasad, M.A., Ph.D., Diploma in Museology
For Agam Kala Prakashan
34, Central Market, Ashok Vihar
Delhi - 110 052
Tel.: 011-27212195, 65688806-7
Fax: 91-11-27212195
Email: agambooks@gmail.com, agambook@yahoo.com
www.agamkala.com

Composed by:
Aman Printographics
Delhi - 110 052
Mobile: 9891395309

Printed by:
Chawla Offsets
Delhi-110 052

Printed in India

ACKNOWLEDGEMENT

It is my pleasant duty to acknowledge the valuable guidance and help I have received from different quarters in the course of this research work. In the first I express my sincerest gratitude and respect to Prof. B.M. Khanduri, Prof. Dinesh Saklani and Sh. S.M. Sethi, Retired Curator Himachal State Museum Shimla without whose constant assistance and guidance it would not have been possible for me to complete in its present form. He was kind enough to go through the manuscript despite his busy schedule and numerous occupations.

I consider it a privilege to express my indebtedness to Sh. M.S. Negi, Curator, Himachal State Museum Shimla, Dr. Balbir Singh Chauhan, former Registering Officer; Sh. Vinay Sharma, Preservation Officer, Himachal State Museum Shimla, Sh. O.D. Bhardwaj, Librarian, Himachal State Museum Shimla for their encouragement and affectionate care. C. L. Kashyap, Archaeological Engineer and Mohammad Latif Malik for making the plans of temples and suggestion.

My thanks are also due to the great scholars in this field from whose work I have been benefited much in course of my research work. I am grateful to the Librarians and their staff members of many libraries including the Himachal State Museum, Shimla, Department of Language and Culture, H.P. Academy of Art and Culture, H.P. State Achieves, Archaeological Survey of India, Indian Institute of Advance Study, Shimla, H.P. University Shimla,

Bhuri Singh Museum Chamba, for their generous help and co-operation. I am very much obliged to all my colleagues and friends in the State Museum Shimla and Ancient History, Culture and Archaeology Department H.N.B. Garhwal University Srinagar, who always extended their help.

The book owes substantially to the thesis, submitted to the University of Hemwati Nandan Bahuguna Garhwal University Sri Nagar in 2008 for Doctor of Philosophy with additions made necessary on account of the onrushing material in the field. The Author craves the indulgence of the readers for errors of omission and commission which might have escaped notice due to my limitation.

HARI CHAUHAN

LIST OF ILLUSTRATIONS

CONTENTS

CHAPTER 1

INTRODUCTION

Geography: The Pabbar Valley consists of the area drained by the river Pabbar and its tributaries in the upper Shimla hills of Himachal Pradesh. The valley extends from the south of Kinnaur to the east of Yamuna valley in Uttrakhand. It is situated in 30°56'26.13° to 31°24'41.08° N and 77° 50'59.20° to 77°59'12.77° E and varies in altitude between 3308 feet to 14506 feet. The Pabbar river rises from the glaciers lake 'Chander Nahan' of the Chanshal peak in the south of Kinnuar and collecting the drainage of the whole tract, it flows south west to Rohru and then turning south east it enters the Uttrakhand and finally merging into Tons River (a tributary of Jamuna) at Tiuni after traveling the distance of 150 km. The principal feeder khad and nallah of the Pabbar are Andhra khad which joins at Chirgaon, Shikri at Rohru, Dougra at Patsari, Bishkulti at Parhat, Shilanti khad at Anu and Anti khad at Anti. Rain and snow are the main source of water rushing from the high peaks which remain covered with snow almost throughout year.

The Valley is connected with the plains of Uttar Pradesh by a state highway running along the right Bank of Pabbar and Tons rivers. The road leading from Rohru to Shimla connects this Valley with the state capital. It lies about 95 km from the state capital Shimla.

Climate: The climate of the valley is moderate and temperature differs in the valley according to their altitudes and geographical locations. The months from April to June are warmer and so are considered as summer months. Monsoon generally sets in July and lasts up to the end of August. Though the tract is surrounded all around by lofty mountains, rainfall is not very heavy. Temperature ranges between 5°C to 40°C in summer to 18°C to 2°C in winter falling drastically with coming of rains in winter. Snowfall occurs during the period of mid of November to April but some high peaks of the valley experience heavy snowfall throughout year.

Flora: The valley has a fascinating flora and presents a variety of vegetation types, ranging between the sub-tropical and the high-alpine. The valley fields and the lower hill slopes are extensively terraced for growing cereal food crop like paddy, maize, sarson, mash, wheat, barley and potato etc. The valley is mainly famed for its extensive apple orchards. The conifers form the most important element in the tree flora forest are covered with dense cover of *chil* Pine (Pinus roxburghie), *kail* (Pinus wallichiana), Deodar (Cedrus deodara), Ban oak (Quercus leucotrichophora), fir etc. The medicinal plants like Tejpata, Dhatura, kubish, banapsha, dhup, pudina, bankakri, patis, mohri, kakarsighi, etc are many herbal types of vegetation growing in the valley.

Fauna: The valley used to abound in a variety of fauna-both beasts and birds, although many species are now becoming extinct because of man's raid on every hill and dale for agriculture, horticulture and habitations. The global warming is no longer a remote threat and soon results into extinction of many species or their migration to safer havens. *Baghera* (leopard), *Kala bhalu* (Himalayan black deer), wild pig, *Ghoral* (hill goat) , *kakkar* (barking deer), *kastura* (musk deer), monkeys are the common sight animals in the forests. Monal, *chukor* (partridge), *Jungli murga* (red jungle fowl), *koyal* (night gale), parrot etc. are some spices found in the valley.

People: People of the area are very simple, god-fearing and peace loving. The population residing in the valley is primarily rural. Ethnically the population is not culturally diverse with almost the entire population being *Pahari* speaking. Although, it was observed and confirmed during the field study, that there is slight variation in the dialect among the population groups from region to region, sometimes within the same area as well. Most of the villagers living in the valley are Hindu by faith. Rajput, Brahmin, Koli, Sunar, Bari (*tarkhan*) and others inhabit the valley. The majority population is of Rajputs. The Rajputs are considered as an offshoot of the Aryans. Rajputs of this area are divided into two groups (1) The Rajputs who were associated with the ruling family of the area are called *Thakurs* and have a higher rank in the society (2) Rajput who formed the fighter race were known as *Khashia* (the great warrior). This fact is also attested by their cultural tradition such as the festival of *'Shant'* (a religious ceremony held for the peace and prosperity of the area) in which they participate carrying their war gear like axes, swords, guns, and many other weapon of offence and defence. They perform their traditional dance brandishing the weapons of their choice and shouting battle cries and slogans of bravery.

According to Gerrald "Khasas have often been referred to as a 'tribal' people. This term has not been defined in such a way as to include satisfactorily the diverse groups. It is often used to designate no to exclude many of the diverse groups it excludes. However, in India it usually refers to peoples who are not Hindu or Muslims or followers of other major religion, who do not have caste organisation, or who practice a more primitive economy than that of most Indian communities. Whatever their origin, the *khasas* of today cannot be considered a tribal people by any of these criteria. They certainly are not aborigines as that term is used in India to denote non-Hindu "original sons of the soil," who live in a "primitive state of existence".[1]

According to Charles A. Sherring, Khasia is that branch of the great Aryan race, which entered India in Vedic times and settled in the Gangetic valley and its surrounding areas.[2] F. E. Pargiter concludes from his research that "tradition or myth indicates that the Ailas (Aryan) entered India from the mid Himalayan region, and its approach toward the N.W. frontier lends no support to any invasion from that quarter".[3] Thus he believes that entry was from Tibet through Garhwal into India.

With the increase of foreign invasion in the Gangetic area they migrated in the hilly areas. According to Grierson "The earliest immigrants (into the *pahari* tract) of whom we have any historical information were *khasas*, They were followed by the Gurjaras, a tribe who invaded India about the sixth century A.D. and occupied the same tract, then known as Sapadalaksha. At that time, they (like the *khasas*) spoke an Aryan, but not necessarily Indo-Aryan language. Of these Gurjaras, the bulk followed pastoral pursuits and merged in and identified with the preceding Khasas population. Others were fighting men, and were identified by the Brahmans with Kshatriyas (warrior class). In this guise they invaded Eastern Rajputana from Sapadalaksha, and possibly, Western Rajputana from Sind, and founded the great Rajput state of Rajputana".[4]

Some Rajputs inhabiting the valley also claim their descent from the Chauhan clan of Rajasthan. Many petty chiefs of Rajput ruled the valley during medieval period but none of them succeeded in establishing supremacy in the entire area. The present ruler of Sirmour has their relationship with the Rajasthan and also the previous clan of Sirmour rulers, who were said to have perished in the flood, their descendent traced their pedigree form the royal clans of Rajasthan. Moreover, there are numbers of people who have migrated from the plains and settled in the hilly region from where they further migrated and settled in the valley still carrying their identity with the previous region.[5] The migration of Rajput from the plain to the hilly region during the Gurjara Pratihars is also established with several references found in various sources. According to Grierson "there was a constant reflux of emigration on the part of the Gurjara Rajput from Rajputana and the neighboring part of India. These re-immigrants became, as befitted their Kshatriya station, the ruler of the country and today most of the chiefs and princes of the old Sapadalaksha trace their descendence from Rajput clan of the plains. The re-immigration was increased by the oppression of the Mughul rule in India proper, and there are historical notices of tribe after tribe, and leader after leader, abandoning their established seats in Rajputana and seeking refuge from Islamic oppression in the hills from which they originally issued to conquer the Gangetic Valley".[6] Hodgson in his account 'The military tribes of Nepal, also states that in event of Mughal invasions in the plains enforced these people to migrate to these hilly regions to maintain their purity of blood and identity.[7]

The second section of the society is the Brahmins. They have the higher rank in the society. They do the priestly work. The Brahmins serve the society in performing the ritual and social rites and get some honorarium in return; however, they are granted with land by the village deity and also have their own land.

Kolis who contribute a large part of population are considered to be the original inhabitant of the area. When the Aryans made advances in the area, they were pushed back, subjugated and assigned to their rigidly inferior social status. For this reason they are sometime included in the account of aborigines. According to Waltson "Domes are the low-caste groups of the Himalayan area they comprise all classes who do menial and more or less degrading duties such as are performed by separate occupational castes in the plains. They are suppressed race, seldom cultivate and practically never own land".[8] But now they have their own land and their economic condition has been improved. The other casts like *Sunar, Bari, Dhaki* also provide their services to support the society in their own ways.

Heritage centres: The Valley is archaeologically rich and the remains scattered all over bespeak the glory and splendor of the area. The region is famous for its ancient stone and wooden temples, which inspired the people to name the Pabbar valley as 'The Valley of Temples'. Many cultural centres flourished in ancient period, which played an important part in the cultural and social life of the people. Hatkoti and Masli, Jubbal, Bachoonch, Rohru, etc are some of famous places known for their rich cultural heritage. In addition to it, every village has a temple of village deity, which plays an important role in their cultural and social life.

Economy: The valley remained economically backward till India attained independence. The petty rulers always kept fighting with each other to establish their supremacy in the area, which hit the economy adversely. The main occupation of the people was cultivation of land and animal husbandry. The land of the area was very fertile and the agricultural yield was very high. Main crops of the region are maize, wheat, barley, rajmash, mash (urad), rice, Potato, and vegetable. Apart from the agricultural land, livestock is the major asset of a large majority of the population. Animal husbandry constitutes the subsidiary occupation for most of the rural folk in general. Every house in the rural area invariably keeps a few cows or buffaloes, sheep, goats and poultry. Animals are kept for milk as well as for other purposes, including as a source of manure for the fields. But with the change of time in the early seventies the people had opted horticulture, which helped to raise the economic condition of the people. This all brought about an economic revolution in the area and raised the living standard and social life of the people. Now the apple cultivation has become the main occupation and people have almost left agriculture. In some areas potato crop has also yielded good results. People sell their horticultural products mainly in Azadpur Fruit Mandi, Delhi and Chandigarh; In addition to these main markets they also export their products to other markets in the country. Consequently the agricultural production has fallen short and the people are depending on the ration shops for food grains. The people have the access to all modern facilities for easy way of life. Rohru is the most suitable market for local people to meet the day-to-day household requirements. To boost the education, a Primary, Middle or a High school has been set up in every village. The area has two Degree colleges at Sarswati Nagar and Seema. The literary percentage is between 75-80%.

Tourism: The valley also has a great potential of eco-tourism. State has been providing opportunity to the lover of like mountain climbing and trekking to long distances and unexplored areas. An adventure sport is being run at Hatkoti by Manali Mountain Institute. The main activity is to organize camps for the adventure lovers from where the cadets climb to the Chanshal peak and river rafting is provided in the Pabbar River.

References:

1. Gerrald D. Berreman, Hindus of Himalayas, p.18.
2. Charles A. Sherring, Western Tibet and the Indian Boarder land, p.61.
3. Pargiter, F.E., Ancient Indian Historical Tradition, 1922, p.299.
4. Grierson, George A. Linguistic Survey of India, p.14.
5. The people of Kathasu village are also known as Chereu. They are migrated here from the Chur area of Chopal and previously supposed to migrate from the plains. The villagers of Bakan are said to be migrated from Bastil area.
6. Grierson, George A. Linguistic Survey of India, pp.14 f.
7. Hodgson- The language, Literature and Religion of Nepal, part II p.37.
8. Walton,H.G. British Garhwal: A Gazetteer 1911a, p.97.

CHAPTER 2

HISTORY

According to a legend, the history of the area began with Mahabharta period.[1] It is believed that Pandavas spent some years of their exile in this region. There are many places associated with Pandavas. Mahabharta also accounts that Pandavas were in exile in the Himalayas after they lost their kingdom in the game of dice has spent few years in this region. According to a legend, the Sunpur Tibba above the Hatkoti was the Sonpur, Capital, and Parhat was the ancient Virat Nagari of Raja Virat where the Pandavas spent a few years of their exile. The place near Rohru is known as 'Lohla Kupri' where a *jatar* is celebrated every year in the memory of Pandavas. Another well-known place in valley is 'Masli' famous for its Pandava temple where the Pandavas with their wife Draupadi are worshiped and a *jatar* is also celebrated in their memory every year. It is believed that Pandava had spent some time in this place. There are many more festivals and folktales associated with the Pandavas. There are some clans of Rajputs i.e. *Sathi* and *Panshi,* who are believed to be the descendent of either the legendry Pandavas and Kauruvas or of their followers and disciples.

The history of the area begins from the early dawn of human civilization. Stone tools discovered at Kalsi,[2] Purola[3] and Tantua Mahadev[4] in the adjoining Yamuna valley reveal that man made his appearance at this part of land in the early Palaeolithic period. But we do not come across any proto -historical find except few terracotta figurines found near Rohru in 1964[5] and in 2006 at Chirgaon some beads were recovered during cutting of road but other objects were destroyed due to ignorance of their importance for the history of the area.[6] PGW were also discovered at Purola in Yamuna valley during the excavation by H.N.B. Garhwal University.[7] Dr. Lalman also reported PGW from the Sirmour area both these valley lies on the periphery of the Pabbar valley.

History of Valley finds some base only with the advent of Maurya dynasty. There are ample references in the *Puranas* and other ancient literature suggesting several tribes inhabiting the Himalayan region. Jain sources state that when Chankya, the Prime Minister of Chandergupta Maurya, failed to uproot the Nanda ruler, he took help from a hill ruler (*pavvo raya*) and besieged Patliputra, and the Nanda ruler had to surrender.[8] However, the hill ruler was killed with the help of a *vish-kanya* to avoid division of the kingdom. Thus, Chandergupta Maurya could also annex the territory of that ruler to his dominion.[9] The extension of Mauryan power in the Himachal Pradesh is also established by the numismatic findings in several parts of Himachal. A hoard of punch marked coins was first reported from Kangra district in AD 1853,[10] and another hoard at Arki[11] in Solan district was found in AD 1969. Yet another hoard is reported from Una and some stray coins from other parts also. [12]

A rock inscription of the Ashokan period found at Kalsi on the bank of Yamuna valley through which a trade route also passes from the plain of Uttar Pradesh to Central Asia along the banks of Yamuna, Tons and Pabbar River indicates the extension of Mauryan Empire in this hilly region.[13] After the downfall of Mauryan dynasty the entire hilly region came under the hill tribes.

After the Mauryas the valley came under the rule of Kuninda tribe, which is attested by the finding of a large number of coins of this tribe in this region. A few years back a hoard of Kuninda coins were found in the Pabbar valley in a small village of Dharmana and Kanot indicating the presence of Kuninda tribe in this region who had inhabited the Pabbar valley for a long period.[14] Alexander Cunningham noticed the sizeable number of *Kunnet* population in the region and he identified them with the Kuninda tribe.[15] Ptolemy refers the country of the Kuninda as *kulindrine*[16] and locates it near the mountainous region where the *Vipasa, Satadru, Yamuna* and *Ganga* have their source. Later, the Kunindas probably merged with the Yaudheya. In the 4th century A.D. Samudragupta in his Allahabad pillar inscription enumerated the Yaudheya, locating them probably along the frontier of his empire but there is no mention of Kuninda. Yaudheya coins were also discovered in the village Panjya in Jaunsar Bawar[17] in Uttrakhand, Nahan, Mandi and Rampur in Himachal Pradesh.[18] Cunningham also reported Yaudheya coins all over the country between Satluj and Yamuna.[19]

In 319-20 A.D. Gupta dynasty was founded in Magadha by Chandragupta I. His son Samudragupta who ascended the throne in 350 A.D., records an elaborate account of his political and military achievement in Allahabad pillar inscription. Inscription refers that the Gupta Empire extended in the north and North West up to Punjab and along with the Himalayan foot-hills.[20] An inscription found at Sunpur Tibba near Hatkoti, which is not deciphered due to its depleted condition records the Gupta script (Pl.1). But there is no other relics found in the area, which can prove that the Gupta rulers either directly or indirectly ruled the area. It seems that when the Guptas were ruling the northern part of India, these tribes still enjoyed the independence, perhaps they were the tribes who were defeated by the Samundra Gupta in his *Dig-Vijay* during his military campaign of Northern India (Aryavrat) and they were permitted to enjoy their independence after paying tribute to the Emperor.[21]

After the down fall of Gupta Empire the northern part of the country was captured by the Harsh the boundary of whose territory were up to

Kashmir.[22] In this period several petty chiefs came in power and set up their rule by acknowledging the imperial power. With the end of Harsha's rule Pratihars rulers extended their empire in the Northern part of India and appointed their Governors in these parts as revealed by the Inscription found on the *torna* of the Durga image at Hatkoti.[23] The temple architecture and sculptural art also held up the influence of Pratihara style in the valley. Pratihara were considered as the patron of art and builder of many temples in the northern part of India. It was during the Pratihara rule that Shankrachrya visited Badrinath. Legend holds that Shankracharya himself founded the temple of Durga at Hatkoti[24]. After the collapse of Pratihara rule the regional governors declared their independence and became the rulers of hilly regions.

The ruler of Sirmour ruled the major part of the Pabbar with his winter capital at Sirmouri Tal and summer capital at Sunpur near Hatkoti in the valley. According to a legend the Raja of Sirmour lost the possession of this area in 1195A.D. under certain adverse condition[25]. The legend is that the Raja presented one of his wives, for a religious act to a *brahmin* Bir Bhatt of local renowance along with the area of Pabbar valley. After the death of Bir Bhatt, the area was divided among his three sons Karam Chand, Mul Chand and Duni Chand. Karam Chand founded the Jubbal State whose capital was Sunpur on the right bank of Pabbar, and was later shifted to Jubbal. Mul Chand got the area of Sari whose boundary extended north of Rampur Bushair up to Nogli. Duni Chand founded the Rawingarh state which was on the left bank of Pabbar and its boundary extended up to the Tons River.[26] But after the devastation of Sirmouri Tal, the area of Sirmour was occupied by the ruler of other clan from Jaislmer and tried to recover the lost region of the state. Malhi Parkash ascended the throne of Sirmour in 1199 A.D. and made his capital at Rajban. He recaptured all the territories belonging to Sirmour but this area came under the Sirmour when Kaul Prakash sits on a *gaddi* (throne) in A.D. 1227. Now these states became the feudatory of Sirmour. In A.D. 1387, Raja Bir Parkash made his capital at Hatkoti and also constructed a temple of Devi and a fort at Rawin and died in 1432 at this place.[27]

According to a legend Raja of Garhwal Ajay Pal (1358-78) over run the trans-Pabbar area and annexed the Rawingarh fort.[28] The trans Pabbar area was under the conflict of Raja of Bushair and Raja of Tehri, Rawin was the fief state of Tehri and was invaded several times by the Raja of Bushair. A treaty was signed between the Raja Pritipati Shah of Garhwal and Raja of Bushair Udai Singh in A.D. 1667(28 *Fagun,Samwat* 1723) not to invade the area of each other and help each other against the outside invasion[29](Pl.2). But some time before the Gurkha invasion the Rawin pargana of the valley was overrun by Bushair forces and seized the fort of Rawin.[30] Rawin chief was Rana Himat Singh. He was helped by Raja Jubbal to retain his hold on the cis-Pabbar portion of the state. He died before the Gurkha invasion.

While the cis-Pabbar was under the conflict of Sirmour and Bushair, Jubbal and Sairi were the tributary of Sirmour state. A treaty was also signed between the Raja of Sirmour Medni Parkash and Raja of Bushair Ram Singh in 1st Shrawan 1738 VS corresponding to A.D. 1681.[31] Sirmour seems to lost their possession over this area during the Gurkha invasion.

In 1810, Gurkahas captured the whole area of Pabbar valley and placed their man Ranjur Thapa, as an administrator of the area at Rawin, and proceeded toward the Rampur by capturing the entire valley. After the declaration of war by the British against the Gurkhas at the end of 1814, the Bushairi force expelled the Gurkhas form their territory and was in combat with Ranjour Thapa at Rawingarh fort when J.B. Fraser arrived at Hatkoti in May 1815.[32] On the final expulsion of the Gurkha, the British took this region under their control and divided the area of the valley between the Jubbal, Rawin, Sairi, Bushair, Garhwal and also retained some part under British.

Rana Puran Chand was granted an independent sanad of Jubbal state and area fall on the south of the valley with its capital at Jubbal. The Rawin State was divided between Garhwal, Rawin and British. A portion of the state east of the Pabbar River was handed over to Garhwal, and was known as Gahrwal –Rawin and Sharachli, Kathasu and Batar was retained under British for some time. The British later transferred this area of their control to Keonthal in exchange of Shimla in 1830.[33] The remaining area which also includes some part of cis-Pabbar was handed over to Rana of Rawin.

Dhadi was also one of the petty states situated on the right bank of Pabbar. Once it was the part of Tharoch Thakurai and later captured by Bushair some time before the Gorkha invasion.[34] It was merged with Rawin State during the Gurkha and later retained by Britisher. In 1853 William Hey declared it a part of Rawin.

According to folklore that Thakur Dharam Singh was the last ruler of Sairi state and was killed in battle in 1813 during Gorkha invasion. He was no son and the state was now under his queen Rani Shringarmungri. Rana Jubbal Puran Chand made many attempt to capture the state but she was helped by Raja Bushair to retain her power over the state but ultimately she accepted the supremacy of Bushair and died in 1864. There was no legal heir of Sairi state and Raja of Bushair, as a suzerain claimed the chief ship as an escheat in default of lineal heir of the late chief and the claim was allowed by British government and was fined with the revenue equal to one year for presenting default claim.

Hatkoti was the main place of religious sanctity in the Pabbar valley. The dispute over the land of Hatkoti became acute in 1886 when Raja Bushair Raghunath Singh started the settlement of his area. Rawin and Jubbal also claimed their possession over this part and Superintendent of Shimla Hill State declared this land a joint property of Jubbal, Rawin and Bushair in 1899 and the dispute was settled for ever.

After Independence, the valley became the integral part of Himachal and Uttar Pradseh (now in Uttarakhand) and falls in Jubbal and Rohru Tehsil of Shimla district and Uttarkashi and Chakrata of Uttrakhand.

References:

1. Chauhan, Jaya., Pabbar-Itihas aivam Sanskriti, p.16.
2. Indian Archaeology (1984): A Review 1961-62, p.103.
3. Tiwari, Rakesh (1984): Exploration Report 1981-82-83, Himalayan Archaeology, Almora, p.123-24.
4. Saklani, P.M. (1994) : Cultural Adaptability in Garhwal Hiamlya, An ethno archaeologicalstudy in Yamuna Valley, Unpublished thesis, Garhwal University, Srinagar.
5. Singh Mian Goverdhan, Himachal Pradesh ka Itihas, p.5 and pt. 4-6.
6. These semiprecious beads were now recovered by Himachal State Museum, Shimla.
7. Nautiyal et. al. Indian Archaeology (1988-89) A- Review , pp. 88-89.
8. Chatterjee, C.D., Early Life of Chandragupta Maurya, B.C. Law Volume-I, p.106.
9. Joshi, M.C., Early History of Himachal Pradesh, Himachal Archaeology-Some aspects, ed. V.C. Ohri, pp.2-3.
10. Cunningham, Alexander, *Catalogue of the coins of Ancient India*, p. XLV; also *Numismatic Chronicle 1853*, p.209.
11. 12 coins are in State Museum Shimla and 25 coins in Bhuri Singh Museum, Chamba.
12. Gupta, P.L., Numismatic History of Himachal Pradesh, p.6.
13. Ibid, pp.5-6.
14. During my research I saw these coins with the local resident Hari Ram and Amar Singh Chauhan.
15. Cunningham, Sir A., Archaeological survey report, 1878-79 p.127.
16. VII, 41, 42.

17. Journal of the Numismatic Society of India, II, pp.109-112,
18. Coins were acquired by Himachal State Museum, Shimla.
19. Cunningham, A., Coins of Ancient India, p.76,
20. Gupta, P.L., Numismatic History of Himachal Pradesh, p.30,
21. Allahabad pillar inscription (Fleet, CII, pp.14ff) mentions that Yaudheya were exterminated by Samundergupta. There is no Yaudheya coin found in the valley so far but it is certain that during the Kushna reign these tribes joined hand to expel them from Himalyan region and Kuninda were merged with Yaudheyas to form a strong hold to fight the Kushana.
22. Puri, Brij Nath, The History of the Gurjara-Pratiharas, pp.57, 71.
23. Himachal Art and Archaeology, Himachal State Museum, Shimla p.34.
24. Singh, Mian Goverdhan, Himachal Pradesh ka Itihas, p.382s.
25. Himachal Pradesh District Gazetteer, Sirmour, p.34.
26. Gazetteer of Shimla Hill States 1910, Jubbal State, p.3.
27. Himachal Pradesh District Gazetteer, Sirmour, p.50.
28. Darshan Bhagat, Garhwal ki Diwangat Vibhutiya, 1952, pp.16-17.
29. Copper plate, State Museum, Shimla.
30. Punjab Government; Punjab State Gazetteer; Shila Hill States-Rawin State, p.1.
31. Copper plate State Museum Shimla.
32. Fraser, J.B., The Himalaya Mountains, p.165.
33. Gazetteer of Shimla Hill States 1910, Rawin State, p.3.
34. Griffin, L.P. Massy; Chiefs and families of the nobles in the Punjab, p.620.

CHAPTER 3

TEMPLES

The Hindu temple is one of the prominent and enduring symbols of its culture. Apart from being a religious institution and place of worship, the temple in India had a hoary past. As a structure that enshrines a god or some other object of veneration. As a religious institution and place of worship they play an important role in the Socio-religious life of the people. The basic elements of the temple and the worship is derived mostly from Vedic and Puranic sources, in course of time the temple assumed different styles and patterns during their diffusion over wide area from the cradle centres of great Indian religions. The form and lay out of these temples depends on the objects of veneration installed and the method adopted for its worship. The craftsman in collaboration with the priesthood determines the forms of the temple with such modification as it fits with the requirements of society and the method of worship.

Due to lack of historical and archaeological data, it is quite difficult to ascertain the antiquity of temple worship although it is a common belief that temple-like structure have been in existence over several millennia. The main reason was that perishable and less durable material such as bamboo, wood, brick and clay only were employed for construction.

In Himachal Pradesh mainly two types of temple exists i.e. Stone and wooden temples. There is no brick temple surviving in the region except for one brick platform discovered in Chamba which belongs to post Gupta period now preserved in Bhuri Singh Museum.[1] A bricks platform was also discovered at Hatkoti in Pabbar valley in the past but due to ignorance the platform was destroyed during cutting of road, only few bricks(80x50x11cm) were recovered by State Museum Shimla and seems to belong to 2nd century A.D. It might not be possible to trace out the architectural style of the temple. It is evident from the numismatic findings that the area of Pabbar valley was inhabited by the Kuninda tribes. In the adjoining area at Purola in the Yamuna valley similar bricks were found in the excavated burnt brick *Vedika(*24x18mete*r)*.[2] The early architectural form of temple are found on the coins of Audumbra discovered from Kangra and its surrounding area depicting simple timber structure with single or multi-storeyed overhanging roof erected over wooden pillars forming an open veranda around the shrine.[3] The stone temple of Mangarh belongs to late Gupta period provide a constant endeavour in the evolution of temple architecture. It is interesting to note that when the stone temple architecture is penetrating in the Himalayan region, the use of wood was also the common practice in temple construction. The Lakshna Devī temple[4] at Bharmour and Shakti Devī temple at Chhatrari are the extant examples of wooden architecture in Himachal Pradesh.

STONE TEMPLES

The stone temples activities in the valley seem to begin with the advent of Partihara rule. No stone temple prior to this era (7th -8th cent.) is noticed in the valley. The earliest stone temple is located at Mangarh (7th cent. A.D.) in Sirmour district. It seems that the temple activities must have started in the area much earlier than the extant structures. The Pabbar valley was once a part of Sirmour and Sunpur at Hatkoti was its summer capital. It is revealed from the inscription engraved on the *toraṇa* of the goddess Mahishasurmardini at Hatkoti temple that the image was cast with the direction of some imperial power. The Partiharas, who were the imperial power during 8th-9th century A.D. in the Northern India, are credited for large number of stone temples in different parts of northern India. It was the period of Partiharas when Shankracharya(spiritual saint of Hinduism) visited Badrinath. The temples of Pabbar valley are much similar to those found at Kullu, Hanol, Lakhamandal, and Jageshwar in Uttranchal and the Central India. There are evidences of more than 25 temples that once existed at Hatkoti the relics of which are still extant. In Bachoonch and Masli large numbers of sculptures and architectural fragments are scattered in its vicinity.

It seems that these temples were destroyed in the political rivalry between the local rulers. It is also attested by the archival records that there was continuous struggle for domination among the rulers of Garhwal, Sirmour and Bushair to capture the area of Pabbar valley[5] while some temples were destroyed in Gorkha invasion. During 19th century A.D some temples also fell prey to inexorable forces of destruction and the ingenuity of man. There were many temples in the surrounding area of Hatkoti till last decade of 20th century signifying the grandeur and beauty of art. Two temples on the left side of Pabbar River just opposite to Parhat temples standing in neglected state were destroyed in earthquake of 1978 A.D. and its fragments are still scattered under the slope of land slide. People living in the surrounding area collected the dressed stone from the site and pile them according to their whim and fancy, it is not possible to trace out the exact architecture of the temples. But from study of architectural fragments and ornamentation and decoration on the surface of the stones it can safely be presumed that these temples were in *nāgara* style coeval with Parhat temples. Another temple which was in good state of preservation by the side of pedestrian path from Hatkoti to Sawra fell prey to vandalism during eighties. A similar example comes from the village Bachoonch where a large *nāgara* temple was destroyed by the Raja of Bushair in the political rivalry and later the same ruler erected the wooden temple in the village to get rid of the curse of the god. The fragments of temples are still scattered in village, though few sculptures collected by the people are now lying in neglected state in the campus of the temple of local deity. From the above evidence, it can be fairly deduced that temple activities in the valley started much before the survived structures of the area. Most of the stone temples of the valley are in *nāgara* style (bearing curvilinear śikhara) and belong to three different phases.[6]

First Phase: In first phase the miniature temples, not more than 2.5 meters high have a single-celled *garbhagṛha* (inner sanctum) preceded by a constricted vestibule (*antrala*) resting on a two octagonal pillars rising from the square base and ending in a rudimentary *ghaṭa pallava* brackets (fig.1). The architectural members as well as the doorways and the pillars are bereft of ornamentation and decoration. The *bhadra* niches contain *purnaratna* decoration and crowned by a small *candraśālā*. The *suknasa* surmounting the pillared portico is profusely decorated with well-chiselled *bhadramukha* and *purnratna* motifs. These shrines are surmounted by the *phamsana śikhara* and topped by āmalaka. Such types of shrines are built at Hatkoti, Parhat and Bachoonch (Pl.3).

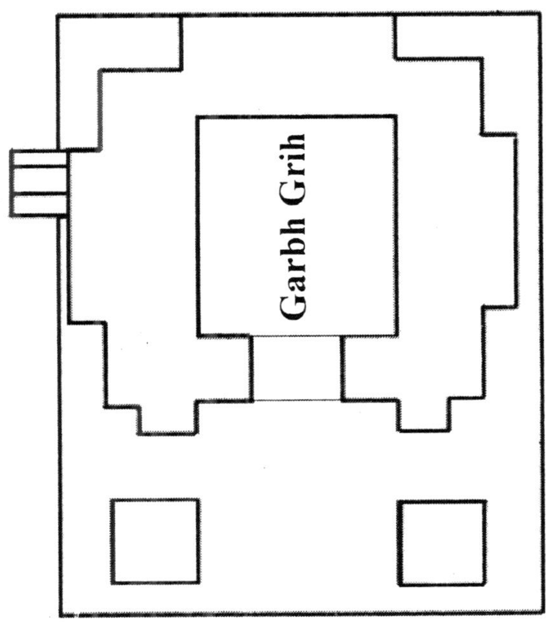

Fig.1. Ground plan of miniature temple, Hatkoti

Second Phase: In second phase, the temples gains height and the *bhadra* projections (wall niches at the cardinal points) are enshrined with finely executed sculptures of the deities. In some temples, *bhadras* are pierced with countersunk niches fronted by two-pillar portico (rathika) harbouring divinities. Architectural designs start appearing, and the pillars, gateways, and *śikhara* are profusely done with *ratana* and *ardha- ratana* (half diamond), spirals and other floral and geometrical designs. Temples are *tri-ratha* (with three offsets) on plan and elevation. In this phase many temple were built but only three examples survive in the valley, two of them stand at Parhat a small village situated at the confluence of Pabbar and Bishkulti rivers another temple stand at Sawra bazaar about one kilometre from Hatkoti and two are standing on the left bank of the Pababr river partly hidden under the shrubs and trees.

ŚivaTemple No.1: The Śiva temple[7] at Parhat represents a distinct phase and by far presents the richest and elaborate technique of temple construction. It is in typical north Indian *nāgara* style and is located on the left bank of the river Bishkulti (Pl.4). The temple today stands forlorn and is hardly visited by the devotees but at one time in history it must have been the centre of cultural activity. The temple is *tri-ratha* in plan and elevation (fig.2). It comprises of *vedibandha*, *jaṅghā* and *śikhara* part. Most of the lower portion of the temple is buried in the ground. So nothing can exactly be known about its base mouldings. It can only be presumed that they are of usual north Indian style comprising *khura, kalsha* and *kapota bandhans*. The *bhadra* part of the temple contains exquisitely chiselled sculptures of Gaṇeśa on the south, Vishṇu on the west and Mahishasurmardini on the north holding their conventional emblems and with their respective vehicles.[8] The *bhadra* niches are crowned by an elegantly chiselled *udgama*. The *karna* terminates with square pilaster (*ardh-stambha*) with *ghata-pallava* at the base and terminating above with the same motif. The recess below is ornamented with bands of lotus petals and on the top with *ardhratnas*. On the top is a cornice running all around the four walls and is decorated with single *candraśālā* motif. A plane *antrapatra* separates this cornice from the first horizontal *kapotapali* tier of the *Śikhara.* The *Śikhara* is of *phamasana* type and comprises 13 *kapotapali*. Śikhara part lies in ruined condition and the *āmalaka* is missing. The door measures 80x 150 cm and has three recessed *shakhas*, the inner most(antra-shakha) and the outermost(bahya-shakha) richly carved with leafy scrolls (vasant paṭṭikā) while the middle (madhya-*shaka*) is decorated with tilka-motif and the architraves carries *ardharatnas*. The *gabvhagrihya* measures 260cm across and enshrines a huge Shivlinga set on a equally proportionate pindika. The façade of the shrine is richly ornamented, the *kapilī* projection surmounted by a *suknasa* sharply ascending but damaged showing a split '*udgama*' its two separate parts enclosing a square niche filled in with an eight armed Nataraja Śiva holding indistinct attributes, an unusual occurrence in the *nāgara* temples of this region .

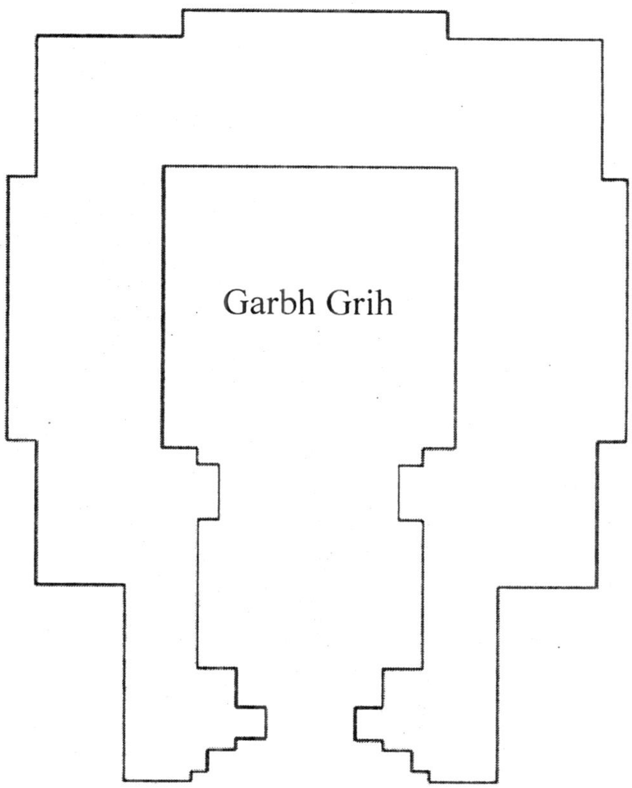

Fig.2. Ground plan of ŚivaTemple, Parhat

Śiva Temple No. II: The temple is located on the right bank of river Bishkutli (Pl.5). The striking feature of the temple are the '*ghanadvaras*' or massive doors breaking through the walls of the *jaṅghā* with their pillared porticos such arrangement found only in few late Gupta temples.[9] The temple rises directly from the ground and is *tri-ratha* in plan and elevation (fig.3). It has simple *vedibandha* mouldings. The *bhadra* on the jaṅghā are pierced with two-pillared portico resting on *manchika* and the fourth side has the entrance door to the *garbhagṛha*. The doorway is surmounted by a *suknasa* of simple variety and topped by the *gavākṣa* shaped *candraśālā* enclosing a lone headed of Maheshwara in its circular medallion. A simple *antrapatra* separates the *Śikhara* from *jaṅghā* portion and bears the motifs of *chaitya*. The *Śikhara* is of *phamsana* type and comprises 28 *kapotālī*. The *śikhara* is without any ornamentation except for some *chaitya* motifs and surmounted by an *āmalaka* and *kalsha* is missing. The sanctum is dark, square and measures 174cm across approached through a door divided in to three plain frames bereft of any decoration. The door measure 73 × 146 cm. A *somsuta* hidden in the floor meant for laving and bathing the *liṅga* appears out side the wall as the *makra* frontage. The temple dates back to early 9th century A.D. on the basis of its architectural style.

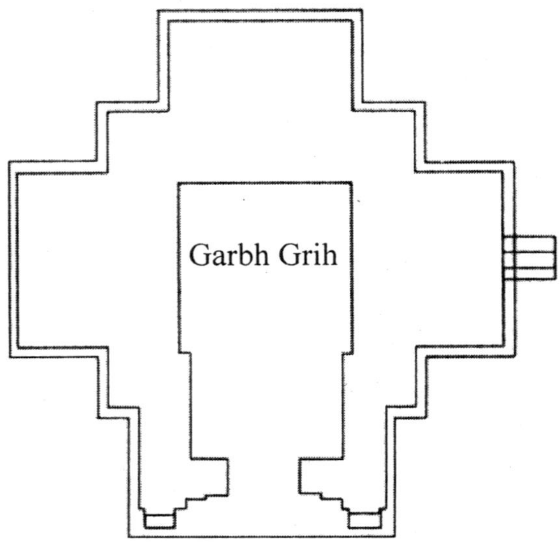

Fig.3. Ground plan, Śiva Temple-II, Parhat

Śiva Temple Sawra: It is situated on the right side of the Pabbar about 1.5 km from Hatkoti at old Sawra bazaar.[11] Temple is *tri-ratha* in plan and elevation (fig.4). Temple is divided into three portions i.e. *Vedibandha, Jaṅghā, Śikhara. Vedibandha* consists of *khura, kumbha, kalsha* and *kapotālī. Jaṅghā* walls are plain having *gavākṣa* windows on three sides (Pl.8). The *jaṅghā* are topped by the eave-cornice decorated with *candraśālā* motifs. The *Śikhara* is of step roof type with fifteen diminishing stages and surmounted by an *āmalaka*. Two square pillars support the rectangular portico in the front. The *garbhagṛha* is rectangular measuring 94cm × 124cm across. The flat roof is covered with a single stone slab. The *sukanasa* has a single *faced bhadra-mukha* on the front.[11] The doorjamb is plain and measure 124cm while the lintel is carved with fine figures of goddess Ganga and Yamuna in *tri-bhanga* posture on either side, flanked by *dvarapalas* and the *uttrang* shows a seated Ganesha. The garbha-griha enshrines a *Śivaliṅga* on a rectangular *pithika* provided with a *pranala* to the north. Architectural style of the temple is datable to early ninth century.

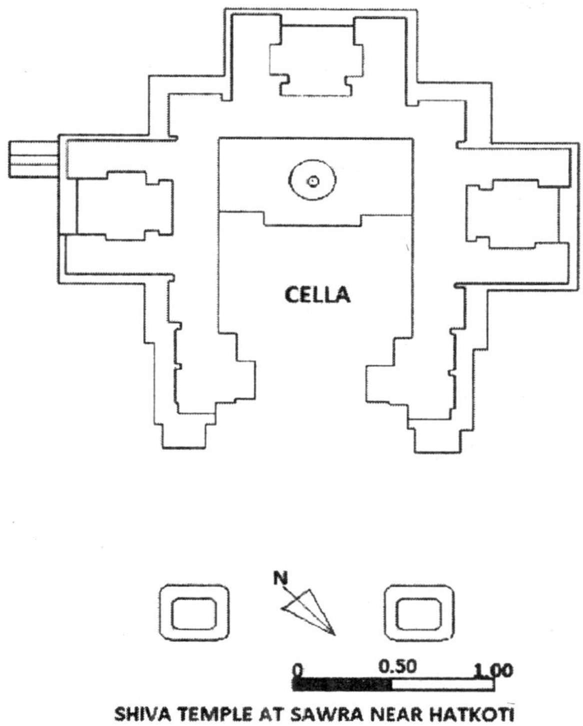

Fig.4. Ground plan, Śiva temple, Sawra (redrawn after L.S.Thakur)

Third Phase: In third phase, temples are built on square platform (jagati), *panch-ratha* (with five offsets) in plan and elevation, and amply provided with *bhadras, pratibhadra* (offset- flanking bhadras), and *Karnas* (angles). Each *karna* is provided with a *bhūmi āmalaka* (cogged wheel marking the storey of a *śikhara*). Temples of third phase are found at Hatkoti in the valley.

Durgā Temple: Temple is situated at Hatkoti a place of great religious sanctity and archaeological importance in the valley. The temple of goddess Durgā is fairly big and is fronted by a large compound; it is the centre of social and religious activities of the region (Pl.6). According to a legend Shankrachrya himself built the temple when he was on his way to Kashmir. The detailed study of the architectural members reveals that the temple was reconstructed in 12th century A.D. and a new *pradakṣiṇāpatha* was added and re-roofed in pyramidal style.[12] J.B. Fraser visited this place in A.D.1816 and mentioned the beauty and fame of the temple complex in his account.[13] Raja Padam Chandra of Jubbal also renovated the temple in 1885. The temple is *panch-ratha* in plan and elevation possessing *bhadra, pratibhadra* and *karna* proliferations. Karnaṣ are marked *with bhūmi-āmalaka.* Temple stands on a raised platform of well-dressed stones, faces east. The sanctum is square and enshrines a life size bronze image of Mahishasurmardini. The door of the sanctum measures 86x170cm, and consists of three receding *shakas* decorated with floral and half-lotus patterns. Figure of Gaṇeśa ardhaparyanka appears on the *lalat-bimba*. The square structure is covered by usual slate roof as pyramid with concave contours and fringes. The slanting roof of slate is topped by *āmalaka* and gold plated *kalsha*. The eaves cornices show fine woodcarvings and are provided with a wooden rattlers at the fringes which emit pleasant sound with the blowing of the mountain wind.

Śiva Temple Hatkoti: The temple is *panch-ratha* in plan and elevation and posses the mouldings of *bhadra, pratibhadra* and *karna* proliferation (fig.5.) The *vedibandha* possess *khura, khumba, kalsha* and *kapotālī.* The whole super structure has been reconstructed at a later date and re-roofed in pyramidal form (Pl.7).. The slanting roof of slate is topped by *chatri, āmalaka. kalsha* and *bijpurka.* The sanctum is dark, square and simple and a large Shiv-liṅga encircled by *yoni-pithika* is installed at the center of the *gabh-agrihya.* An interesting feature of the temple is exquisite woodcarving at its ceiling.

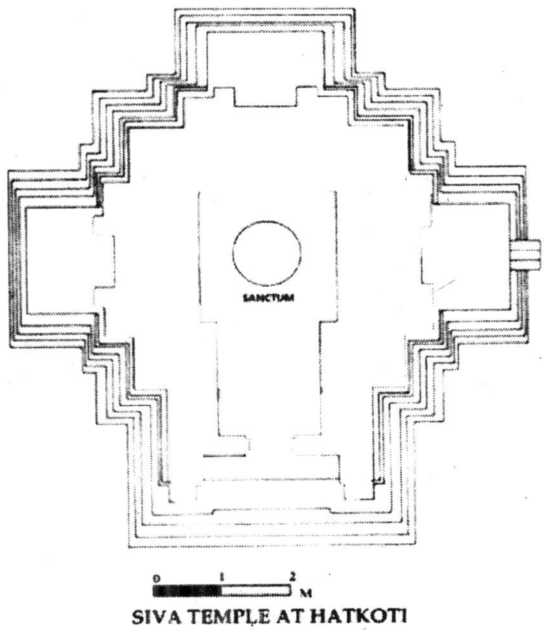

Fig.5. Ground plan, ŚivaTemple, Hatkoti (redrawn after L.S.Thakur)

WOODEN TEMPLES

The valley experiences very heavy rain and snow fall which forced the architects of the temple to construct the wooden structure to protect the devotees from cold and slanting roofing for their long life. These temples are not only the focal points of its religio-cultural activities and beliefs of the peoples, but also the veritable repositories of the religio-artistic expression of the plastic art of the people. Wooden temples which evolved from remote antiquities, were just platforms open to sky with some kinds of an iconic representation, which could more accurately be named *'sthan'*, or *'thada'*. There were such shrines of *Jagah*(earth goddess)and of *Beer*(minor deities)Pl.9. The second stage was reached when a small structure of stone and wooden planks were raised to save the symbols of deities from climatic condition and vandalism known as *'Chaunra'*(Pl.10). In the third stage the temple size increased considerably and it became a single or multi-storeyed structure known as *'deuthi'* or *'deul'* where the principal deity is enshrined in the *garbhgriha*.

Material : The valley is infested with different type of flora and fauna and served as a favourite medium not only for the construction of dwelling but also for the edifices of more ornamental character like temple. The wooden temple is considered as indigenous in origin and scattered in every part of the valley. However the survived example hardly extends beyond 17th century A.D. because of its perishable nature. The wooden temple which is suitable in the environmental condition prevailed in these hilly region supports its existence from very early time. Wood is widely used for construction and embellishment of temples, as is easily available and readily tractable material. Deodar being the wood par excellence (Dev-daru, the wood of the gods) is usually employed in the temple. These temples, built like most of the other buildings of that material are immense in form, but at the same time are more picturesque and richly carved.

It is generally believed that wood was used by the Indus people. The Rig Veda attests the popularity of wood in the next phase of culture.[14] The Rig Vedic hymnist in one place asks: 'which was the forest and what was the tree out of whose wood the heaven and earth was carved' It was the wood that first came to the mind of the Vedic sage in the creation of the universe by the Vishvakarma. There are several references in the epics about the wooden object and carvings. The reference related to wooden palace of the Mauryan period at Patliputra (Patna), are found in the classical accounts. Historian have noted that the palaces of the great Mauryan Emperor Chandragupta at Patliputra which surpassed in splendour the royal residence of Susa and Ekbatana were made of wood and the remnants of buildings discovered at the Mauryan sites such as Bulandigarh and Kumrahan in Patna have confirmed the literary evidence.[15] The stone temples and caves are considered as imitation of wooden structures as revealed from various ancient structure. The sculptural relief of Sanchi, Bharhut etc. portray the copies of wooden building which were common in ancient time. The style with which the stone media has been treated so as to erect pillar, carve out friezes and architraves and build up the facades and *toraṇa* reflect the translation of wood-carving technique into stone. The valley is inhabited by people belonging to different class of society right from very beginning, were the followers of Hinduism and worshipped the divinities in anthropomorphic form and built the structure for its worship, the evidence of such structure came as a fragment of brick platform found at Hatkoti.[16] In the Audumbra coins one can find the depiction of double story temple which appears as a wooden structure.[17]

The earliest surviving specimen of wooden temples exists at Bharmour and Chhatrari in Chamba district. Temple of Lakshna Devī at Chaurasi temple complex and Shakti Devī temple at Chhatrari datable to 7th -8th century A.D., are still intact and in the best state of preservation give us some insight of prevalence of wooden architecture in the Himalayan region.

Architecture: The wood is used traditionally to impart stability to the structure. The walls of these temples are raised on the horizontal wooden framework called *cheols* (wooden beam) and consist of alternate course of wood and stone at right angle. In the well-built structure, the wood is very carefully arranged and extending over the whole length of the wall. The end of the beam are slightly let into each other and a small piece of dove-tailed wood are further inserted in between each of the two beams to prevent them from bulging out by the pressure of the stone.

The wall construction technique applied in the temple is mainly of two types: a) wall containing alternate rows of stones and wood and are know as *katth-kuni* b) wall containing multiple course of stone between the two rows of beam(*cheole*) known as *dhole-maidgi* wall.

It was Captain A.F.P. Harcourt who first took note of the architectural grandeur of the wooden temples of Kullu and classified it on basis of roof form[18] and later Penelope Chetwode studied the Hindu architecture of western Himalayas and divided into five main groups.[19] Her classification is mainly based on Harcourt classification and only added one new type which she noticed in Satluj Valley and termed it as 'Satluj valley style'(consisting of a maṇḍapa with one or more pagoda roofs above *garbha-griha*. Her classification is as:

1. The classical stone Śikhara style
2. Pent-roofed style
3. Chalet style
4. Pagoda style
5. Satluj valley style

But O.C. Handa in his book *Temple Architecture of the Western Himalaya, wooden temple*, broadly classified the wooden temples in seven categories[20] on their elevation characteristic and roof form as:

1. Gable-roofed temples
2. Composite-roofed temple
3. Tower temples
4. Multi-tiered Pyramidal temple
5. Canopied Composite –roofed temple
6. Circular-roofed temple
7. Composite temple

To study the temple architecture of the valley the above classification is more suitable to classify the temple and could be divided into four main categories based on roof style (1) Pent roof comparable to gable roof(2) Pyramid type (3) Pagoda type (4) Pent-n-gable type comparable to composite temple.

I. Pent-roof: The pent roof temples are peculiar to the valley. The rectangular (exceptionally square) wood and stone temple with pent-roof seems to the most ancient.[21] The temple is usually a rectangular in plan and stand on a low platform of stone. The use of wood and its arrangement with stone is one of the marked features of these temples. The wall of the temples consists of the alternative course of wood and stone. In some cases there are many courses of stone between the wooden beam (*cheole*) which is laid horizontally on the wall and such walls are known as *dhol-maidgi*. Some time mortar is also applied to binds the layers of stones to strengthen the wall. It generally consists of a central cella with an open veranda and a door in front. In case temple is multi-storeyed, the veranda serves as a circumambulatory around the four walls of the building. The whole structure is covered with a pent-roof of stone slate, which slopes on two sides from a central ridge. The angles of roof depend on the arrangement of the row of planks being raised slightly to give a greater dip to keep out water and snow. The pointed roof is surmounted by a heavy ridge beam locally known as *kurd*. The roof which overhangs the structure rest on beams which projects from the wall. The eaves of the temple are covered with carved planks and in those are fitted the wooden bells by nails. The door-jams, lintel and facades are decorated with carvings depicting devices like snakes animals, bird's foliage and geometrical designs etc.

II. Pyramidal style: The temples are built on square or rectangular plan usually on low plinth of rough stones. First two wooden beams (*cheol*) are laid along opposite sides on outside and another inside. Another beam are laid on right angle above it, the intervening spaces being filled-up with dressed stone. On these again rest the next set of beam and in this way building rises course by course. All the four lower eaves of the temple roof are of equal length and then the roof goes on narrowing towards the centre forming a pyramid-like roof in the centre, with a *chhatri* (canopy) and *kalsha* on the top.

III. Pagoda Style: The pagoda style is one for which histories of Indian art use various regional terms, though in this Himalayan region, it simplifies the matters if one stick to the familiar term pagoda, by which it meant a building with a succession of superimposed pent-roof, each one is little smaller than the below it. The rest of the characters of the temple are same as in pent roof.

IV. Pent-n-gable type: It is a composite style of roofing of the temple. The roof of the temple is divided into two parts. The veranda of the temple is covered with pent type roof while the sanctum is covered with gable type.

Mahasu devata temple at Badiyar: Mahasu devata temple Badiyar is situated about 10 Km from Hatkoti in the spur of Pabbar valley. The temple is two storied and consists of alternative layers of stones and wooden beams on right angle (Pl.11). The space is filled with the dressed stone. The ground floor consists of a two compartments (fig.6). The outer serve as a rest room for the priest and devotee while the inner compartment serves the purpose of store. The first floor is approached through an internal stepladder. This story also contains two compartments. The inner room serves as sanctum-sanctorum where the deity is placed with the religious artefacts and the outer porch is used for sitting purpose. The temple is roofed in pyramidal style and *chhatri* and *kalsha* is placed at the top. Such roof is also known as bhima-chhatri type because of roof style of great goddess Bhima kali temple, Sarhan. The entrance door of the temple is profusely carved. The doorjambs show the figure of minor deities on either side and their names-*Kaulu* and *Narsing* are carved below. Since they usually guard the outermost entrance to a temple compound and capture the visitor attention first. The being thus chosen to stand in external protection are known for their physical strength and for their ferociousness, these guardians keep evil spirits from entering the precincts and frighten the unbeliever. The lintel is carved with the image of Gaṇeśa in the centre along with his mount rat and ends are carved with the lion's heads known as *sihmukh*. The horizontal beams of the frontal part of the temple are carved with interlacing snakes and floral patterns, adding to the beauty of the temple. The wooden bells of 5-6 inches in length are suspended beneath the edge of overhanging roofs all around temple. They are attached to the lower edge of eave planks by small a hook which catches every wind and cause the bell to sound musically in the breeze. These small bells are meant to invoke the god through their sound. They call the devotees to visit the temple and they send the devotee's prayers to the realm of divinity. There are two small temples in the campus dedicated to its beer and roofed in pent-roof style.

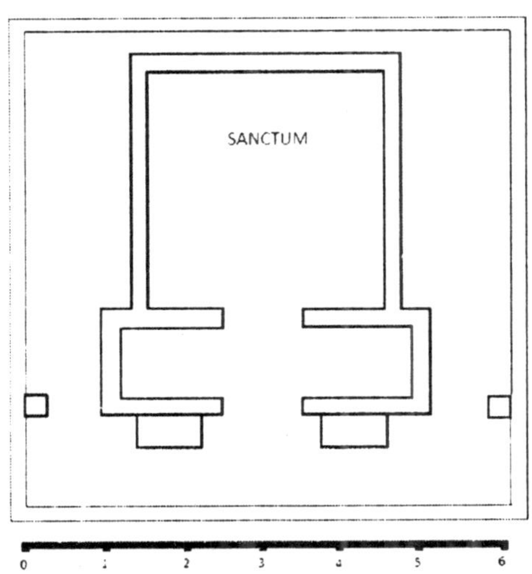

Fig.6. Ground plan of Mahasu devata temple, Badiyar

Kainlu Devata temple Rohtan: Temple is situated in the outskirt of the village Rohtan in the forest on the left side of the river Pabbar. Temple is very ancient but renovated many times. The temple is of great antiquity due to its roof arrangement (Pl.12). Temple stands on the high plinth of dressed stone. The walls of temple consist of alternating rows of stones and wood and have a sanctum sanctorum (garbhgriha) and a porch on its front which is covered with wooden planks to ensure the security of the temple (fig.7). Temple is roofed in pyramid style but to make it more ornamental and impressive another roof is superimposed on the apex. The roof is topped by *chhatri* ant *kalasha*. Fringes are provided with hanging wooden bells.

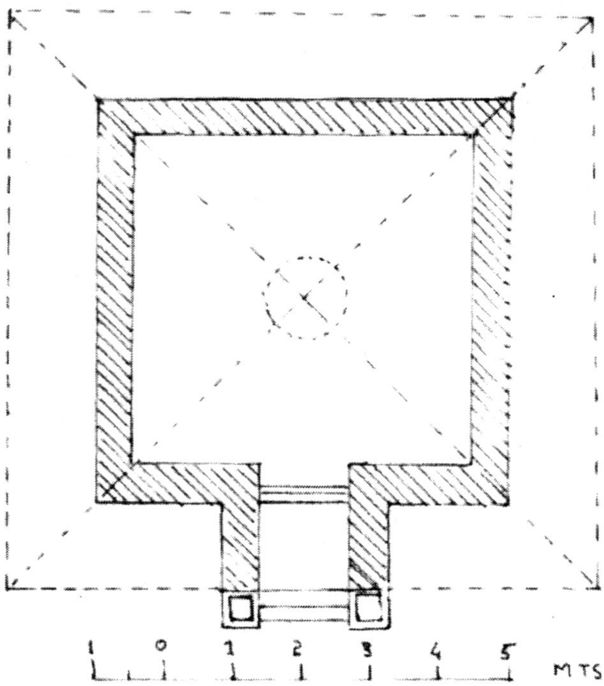

Fig.7. Ground plan of Kainlu Devata temple, Rohtan

Banar-Devta temple at Pujarli: Pujarli village is the main seat of Banar-Devta, one of the known local deities of Pabbar Valley. The temple lies about 15 Km away from Hatkoti on the left side of the river Pabbar. The temple stands as magnificent example of tower type temple (Pl.13). The multi-storied superstructure stands on a high plinth of dressed stone and built in alternating layers of stone and timbers. In order to ensure the stability of structure the horizontal wooden beams are laid on at the top of other. The mesh, thus created was filled with dressed stone. For approaching the first floor stepped wooden ladder is provided from the ground. The veranda serves as an ambulatory. The outer edges of the veranda are supported by well-carved wooden post (fig.8). The gaps between the posts are filled with semi-circular well-carved arches, composed by the curvilinear combination of small cusped arches. One can enter the temple by stepped ladder from the ground to the veranda and through entrance door '*Kholi*' (sacred entrance door) public enter inside the temple from where a stepped wooden ladder passes internally and reaches in the projected balcony and then enters into the sanctum sanctorum. The temple is roofed in Pagoda style. The eaves planks are richly carved with folk motifs and floral and geometrical patterns.

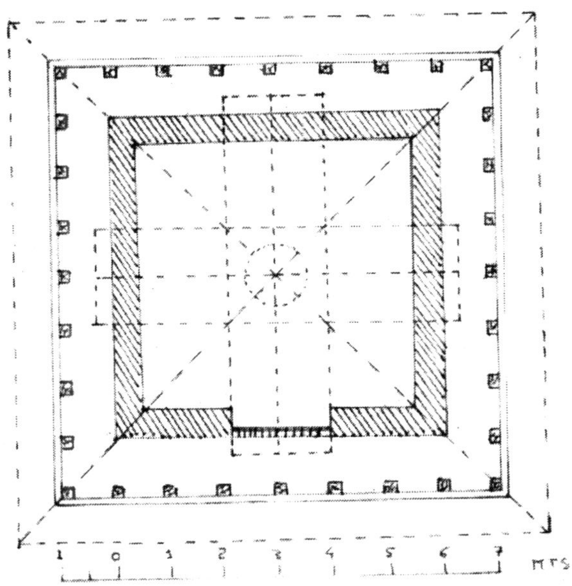

Fig.8. Ground plan of Banar-Devta temple, Pujarli

Bondra temple at Bachoonch: Banchoonch is a small village on the Rohru-Summerkot road at the right bank of river Shikri, a tributary of river Pabbar about 15 Km from Rohru in district Shimla of Himachal Pradesh. The village has temple of local deity Bondra.[22] The scattered sculpture shows that this place remains the seat of Shaiva and Sakta sect during the 10th- 11th century A.D. The ancient temple was damaged by the Raja of Bushair State some time back in 18th century AD. Later, the same ruler gott rid of curse of the deity and built this temple again. He called the masons from Mandi and built the temple in Pent-n-gable style. The temple is built of dry stone masonry with wooden beams at the wide interval for the strengthening of the wall and horizontals beams of wood are laid on wall dividing the stories of the temple from inside. The passage for these storeys is from inside and are used only for specific purpose. The lowermost story serve as room for ritual purpose where a *Havana-kund* is built and the upper stories serve as the purpose of storage of grain presented by the people at the time of every harvest(fig.9). An external ladder is provided from the stone-paved courtyard to the ground floor, through a cantilevered balcony. The top floor is approached through internal stepladder. The temple is roofed in a very

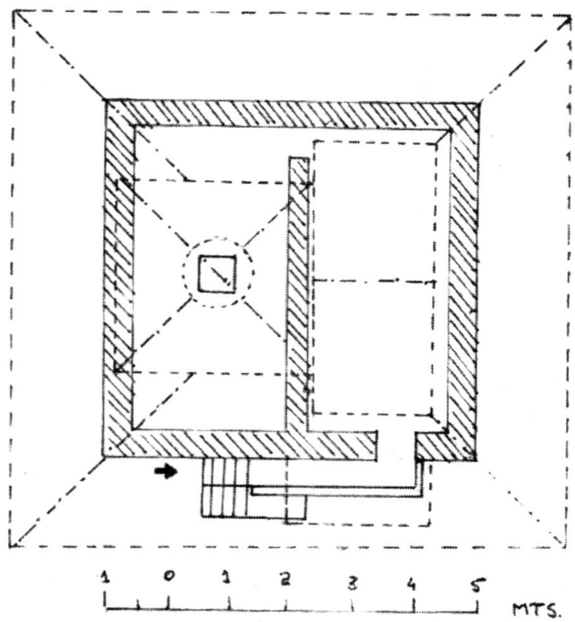

Fig.9. Ground plan of Bondra temple, Bachoonch

elaborate manner, which elevated wooden framework to prop up the roof structure, which gives an impression of another story above the sanctum. However, it is all ornamental roofing arrangement. The roof-proper is laid in composite pent-n-gable manner, and is richly decorated.

Reference:

1. Vogel, J.Ph. , *Antiquities of Chamba, part I*, p.20.
2. Nautiyal, K.P. Khanduri, B.M., Excavation of a Vedic brick altar at Purola, district Uttarkashi, Central Himalya, *Purattava*-11, pp.68-69.
3. Thakur, L.S., *The Architectural Heritage of Himachal Pradesh*, p.27.
4. Vogel, J.Ph., *Antiquities of Chamba*, p.7.
5. Two copper plates preserved in State Museum Shimla indicate continues struggle between Rampur, Sirmour and Garhwal rulers to occupy the Pabbar valley.
6. Chauhan, Hari, Hatkoti, a place of religious sanctity, *Marg Magzine* No.53 vol.3.
7. Thakur, L.S., *The Architectural Heritage of Himachal Pradesh*, p.50.
8. Same order is observed at the Bajaura temple at Kullu.
9. Baijnath temple also shows similar arrangement.
10. Thakur, Laxman S., *The Architectural Heritage of Himachal Pradesh*, p.50.
11. Bhardramukha member dislodged was transferred to Himachal State Museum Shimla during the research by present scholar.
12. *Gazetteer of Sirmour*, p.50.
13. Fraser, James, *Himalaya Mountain*.
14. X.81.4.

15. Brown, Percy, *Indian Architecture, (Buddhist and Hindu)*, p.6.
16. A brick structure was found near Hatkoti during the cutting of the road, some bricks of the structure are now preserved in Himachal State Museum Shimla and seems to belong to 2nd century A.D.
17. Saran, M.K., *Tribal coins-A study.*
18. Harcourt A.P.F., *The Himalayan District of Kooloo, Lahul and Spiti*, reprint, 1972, p.60.
19. Chetwode, Penelope., Hindu Architecture in the Western Himalaya, p.166, *Arts of Himachal,* Himachal State Museum Shimla.
20. Handa, O.C.,*Temple Architecture of the Western Himalaya, wooden temple.*
21. Bandaranayake, Senake, The recovery of a 'lost Architectural Style': some roof forms from the Ajanta Mural and related material, *Madhu-Recent Research in Indian Archaeology & Art History.*
22. Handa, O.C., *Temple Architecture of the Western Himalaya, wooden temple*, p.214.

CHAPTER 4

SCULPTURES

The sculpture may truly be regarded as the characteristic art of the area in which the genius of the people found its concrete, lasting and full expression.[1] Sculptures not only serve the religious purpose of the people of that period but also reflect their spirit, tradition and creative impulse. These sculptures are carved out either in stone, wood or caste in metal. The temples built in the area possess abundant sculptures of great variety and beauty, often marked by monumental quality. According to K.M. Munshi "In India, Art founds its home in the temple which was not only the physical core, but the soul of the community... The shapes and forms of its sculptures and the colour of its walls only recorded the heartbeats and the spiritual aspiration of a vigorous racial life."[2]

The art of sculpture was practised by the people of India from very ancient times. Many specimens of different kind of figures, both animal and human, belonging to the pre-historic and proto-historic ages have been found in various parts of the country. The materials used at first were generally impermanent like wood and clay and rarely of a more durable material like stone and metal. As wood does not last for a long time due to its perishable nature hence no early wooden sculptures have been found. But clay figurines burnt in fire have been discovered in large numbers and the represents the attempt of Indian sculptors in the field of plastic modelling and composition. Numerous terracotta figurines and a few partially preserved stone and bronze figures of the early Indus valley sites show a high state of proficiency, which suggests a very earlier development. The perfection in modelling of figure and the technical skill of the craftsman who could cast images in metal and fashion them with ease in clay give us a picture of the artwork of that civilization.

Stone is most durable material used for sculptures by the sculptor to express their artistic expression. The majority of sculptures are found in stone and were generally used for the embellishment and worship in the *nāgara* temples. The post Gupta period which is also known as Rajput period (8th –12th century A.D.) is the classical period of the sculptural art of the Himachal Pradesh. It was under the Gurjara Partiharas that this art attained the height and a number of incarnations of deities were incorporated in the form of sculptures. The sculptural activities seem to gain strong hold under Yashovarman of Kannauj in 8th century. With the first half of 8th century, we reach the last phase of Gupta art tradition which we may connect an invasion of early Kashmiri style as reflected in Vaikuntha images. The Kashmiri influence can be traced from Bharmour, Chamba, Baijnath in Kangra, Bilaspur, Naggar and Manali in Kullu and even in Udaipur and Trilokinath in Lahul. These sculptures are characterized by smooth plasticity of Gupta canon blended with the Kashmiri crowns of *trikaṇtka* variety, physiognomy powerful and full of vitality with bellies pronouncly modelled.

The Sculptures of the Pabbar valley reveal that they possess the stylistic sophistication of post-Gupta period. The figures of god and goddess have hypnotic expression in their eyes with gently arched eyebrows, soft smile, and dignified expression on the marvellously rounded faces. These sculptures show their close resemblance with the sculptures of Gangetic plains. A trade route leading from plains of Uttar Pradesh to Central Asia passing through this valley is the main factor for spreading this art-style in the region.[3] The contents of these sculptures, although most varied, mainly revolve around two subjects: (a) Brahmanical pantheon with images and legendry scenes of gods and goddess (b) decorative figures, motifs and designs. The family of *Brahmanical* gods and goddesses, although formidable in size, can be conventionality grouped around the personality of the five principal deities, namely *Śiva, Vishṇu, Sūrya, Gaṇeśa and Durgā.* They are represented either singly or attended by their consorts and attendants. Deities are also shown accompanied by a number of celestial beings. In sculpture, much attention has been paid to the life-exploits of each deity in various incarnations showing his victory over a number of demons.

1. Śiva: Śiva is one of the important member of the Brahmanical triad, has been worshiped since the proto-historical period.[4] Śiva is one of the most important and popular deities in the valley both in the past and present. He is represented in the sculpture in two forms, aniconic and anthropomorphic. Aniconically, he is represented in the form of liṅgas. The earliest reference of Śiva liṅga occurs in the Bauddhayana Grhyasutra.[5] However, the earliest representation of liṅga occurs on a lintel belonging to c. 1st century B.C. exhibited in Mathura Museum (no.52, 3625).[6] According to A.M. Shastri the human figure of Śiva first appears on Kada Coins with *daṇḍa* and *kamaṇḍalu*. It is the earliest representation of Śiva in human form so far as the historical period.[7] In anthropomorphic representation he is represented as sthānaka Śiva, Umā Maheśvara, and Naṭarāja etc.

Śiva: A stone sculpture from Bachoonch represents four armed Śiva following the Kidra Kushāṇa iconography except for the bull Nandī seated in relaxed posture behind Śiva(Pl.14). Śiva is standing in *samabhaṅga, Sampada* and *sthānaka* posture.[8] The deity is shown with *jaṭāmukuṭa, kuṇḍalas, rudraksha-mala.* He wears a knee length dhoti held at the waist by a girdle with a clasp in form of lotus rosette. He holds a trident in the front right hand and most probably a *kamaṇḍalu* in the back right hand. He is holding of a snake by the head in the back left hand while the attribute in the front hand is indistinct and is broken. Most probably, he holds a *kapala* in this hand. The sculpture may be assigned to 10th -11th century A.D.

Naṭarāja: Śiva in another form in the valley find representation as Naṭarāja. This form of Śiva is found on the *śuknāsa* of Śiva temple at Parhat and belongs to 8th century. It is perhaps the most widely known aspect of Śiva as the 'Lord of Dance' The whole cosmos is his theatre and his dance is symbol of his five divine activities of creation, preservation, destruction, illusion and release.[9] Creation arises from the ḍamru, which is the symbol of vibration and is held in the upper right hand, Protection is assured by the lower right hand, which is held in *abhya mudrā*. The upper left hand points to the raised leg which gives release from all bonds. The leg that crushes the demon Muyalaka is the refuge for tired souls that seek escape from causality. The encircling arch '*prabhāmaṇḍala*' which spring from the Naṭarāja image represent nature that is inert which Śiva galvanises into activity. He dances with fire, water, ether and wind. 'Dancing, he sustain the manifolds phenomena. In the fullness of time, still dancing, he destroys all forms and names by fire and gives new rest'.[10]

Umā Maheśvara: Stone sculptures of Śiva-Pārvati seated on Nandī are also noticed in large number in the valley. A Stone sculpture of an *aliṅgan mūrti* of Śiva is noticed at Hatkoti temple complex. In this image Śiva sits in *lalit-sayya-asna* on a bull Nandī while Uma sits in *vamlalita asna* on the left thigh of his master. Śiva embraces Umā (aliṅga) by throwing his left natural arm around Umā and Umā turns her face lovingly towards him and is known in the text *Har-Vaktra-Abilokini*.

2.Vishṇu: The god par-excellence of *Bhāgavatās*, is one of the supreme deities in Hindu Pantheon. He is considered as the preserver and upholder of the universe and is the great guardian of the Law of Dharma. Whenever unrighteousness triumphs and the rhythm of the universe is disturbed he manifests himself in the world and redeems it from its woes. He is worshipped among the masses in his various forms. Since the valley is dominated by the ancient Śiva and *Śakti* cult. There seems to be no independent temple dedicated to Vishṇu in any form, however, his sculptures are noticed in association with the sculptures of other deities in various temples. The valley possesses some rare and interesting Vishṇu images executed with great artistic skill. According to the canon of *Śilpśatras*, the images of simple form of Vishṇu may be divided into Śayana, Sthānaka and asana respectively.

Sthānaka mūrti: A *sthānakamūrti* of Vishṇu set against a plain rectangular stella is found at Bondra temple complex.[11] It is rounded at the top and embossed with plain circular nimbus(Pl.15). The figure is shown in a strict frontal stance. Vishṇu is wearing high crown *Kirīta mukuṭa* and other ornaments are arranged beautifully on his body. He is holding his usual attributes. Markandeya and Bhu Devī are standing on either side in accentuated in *tri-bhanga* posture in sharp contrast to the main figure. Two squatting figures are shown on either side at the upper corner. The sculpture was partially damaged in the fire. According to T.A.G. Rao " This form is the best fitted to have the temple thereof constructed within town and villages, as it is conceived to be the giver of all happiness to its worshipper and has therefore to be worshipped and prayed to by all sorts of men and women belonging to all condition of life."[12]

Śayana: Another sculpture of Vishṇu in *Śayana* form is noticed in the Śiva temple at Hatkoti temple complex. This form of Vishṇu is to be assumed by the deity with in the sea at the end of great deluge of universal dissolution. The deity is shown reclining gracefully on the great serpent Ananta(Eternity) also called *Ādi Śesha*, whose hoods are spread over his head. The Lotus stalk seen emerging from his navel and rest of details are badly eroded and not visible. The sculpture is tentatively dated to 12th century A.D.

Vishṇu maunavrtin: Another rare sculpture of Vishṇu in *āsna* form is noticed in the niche of the platform of Durgā temple at Hatkoti (Pl.16). The deity is shown seating in Kushana style (Utkuṭikāsana) on *tri-ratha* pedestal while the back slab is semi circular at the top. He is shown wearing *kirīta mukuṭa*, long kuṇḍalass, *ekāvalī* and the ends of dhoti are gathered in between the legs and are without any folds. He is holding conch in back right hand and front natural hand is held in *varda mudrā* while his right backhand is holding *chakra* (disc) with a ribbon issuing from its axis reminiscent of the Gurjara-Pratihara sculptures of this region and front left hand is placed on the mouth instructing silence(maun). The god seems to insist on silence and tranquillity so very necessary for concentration by this characteristic *mudrā* . This form of god is known as Vishṇu maunavrtin. The sculptures of this form are very rare and only sculpture of this kind is noticed at Khajuraho where the god is seen seating in *padmāsna* and his index finger of front left hand is shown touching the left corner of the lip.[13] On the basis of iconographic traits the sculpture may be assigned to c.6th –7th century A.D.

Garuḍasin Lakshmī-Nārāyaṇa: Vishṇu is also shown with Lakshmī seated on the Garuḍa in *āliṅgan mudrā* and is known as Garuḍasin Lakshmī-Nārāyaṇa. In such type of sculpture Lakshmī is shown seated on the lap of his spouse and embracing him. There are many sculpture of this kind noticed at various places in the valley. One such type of sculpture carved on rectangular stella with semi circular top, is placed in the Śiva temple Hatkoti (Pl.17). In this sculpture Lakshmī-Nārāyan is seated on the shoulder of kneeling and striding *Garuḍa* (personified in human form) with folded hands. The *Garuḍa* is seen looking up at the wonder of the lord Vishṇu (Deva-vi- Kashna-Tatpra). The four-armed deity is seated in *lalitasna* with one leg bent and other is placed on the lotus cushion on the pedestal. The deity holds a lotus and a mace in the right hands while the disc and conch are shown in the left hands. Lakshmī is holding a bud of the flower (lila-kamal) in the left hand resting on thigh and embracing the god with right one. Her left leg is also placed on the long stalked lotus cushion. The back of the slab is perforated. Miniature sculptures of Brahma and Śiva are carved on the left and right side on the top and act as *pārśvadevta* and to indicate the supremacy of Vishṇu as *Mūlanāyaka*. A pettalled lotus is embossed in the centre as *prabhā*. Two miniature figures probably devotees with folded hands are kneeling at the feet and behind them are two standing female figures. Two prancing Sardul are seen on either side of the back slab. In the upper part of the *toraṇa* are seen *maladharas* with open garlands flying towards what looks like to be a crown. Such an arrangement was the popular with the Gurjara-Pratihara of this region as seen in the door jamb of the Rangnath temple of Bilaspur (8th century A.D.), Lakshna Devī temple of Bharmour(7th century A.D.) and rock cut temple of Masrur, Kangra (8th Century A.D.). The stone image on stylistic ground and iconographical traits is dated to c.10th –11th century A.D.

Sūrya: Sūrya, one of the five principal gods of the Brahmanical pantheon, has been worshipped in India from the very early times, initially in an aniconic form and later in iconic form.[14] But it received a new turn with the advent of Maga Brahmins, the sun-worshiping priest from Iran in the early centuries of Christian era. In the Gupta period the lord of light became the part of the Hindu trinity.[15] Sūrya sculptures are very rare in the valley. A detached stone sculpture of Sūrya is noticed at Bondra temple.[16] He is shown standing along with two miniature attendants *Daṇḍa* and *Piṅgala* on a raised pedestal (Pl.18). His charioteer Aruna is shown at his feet. The deity is holding full-blossomed lotus in both the hands rising up to the shoulders (*skandha-desha*) as usually seen in the Sūrya sculptures of North India.

The image is fully Indianised and is shown wearing Indian dress instead of Iranian wearing. The upper part of the body is without the usual armour though he is shown wearing trousers and short boot. The *uttriya* is worn like a *vaijantī* coming upto the ankles and the ends of the *uttriya* resting over the arms. The deity is embellished with *kirtimukuta*, *prabha-mandala*, ear rings, girdle, beaded *yajñopavīta* and armlets, arranged tastefully on his body. The treatment of body is quite sensitive to meet the iconographical requirement. The figure is shown standing in a strict frontal pose (sambhanga) but the two attendant's figures with their triple bend are in contrast introducing as they do a rhythm in the composition. The face is somewhat conical with ridged eyebrows, curved eyelids, small chin and a stubby nose. The lips are full and sensitive. On the lower left *Daṇḍa* is shown with spear and on the lower right *Piṅgala* is shown with pen and inkpot. On the stylistic ground, the sculpture can be ascribed to 12th century A.D. Another stone sculpture of Sūrya is noticed at Hatkoti in Durgā temple and shows similar features but the sculpture is somewhat earlier and belongs to 10th –11th century A.D.

Devī: In Hindu pantheon, *devī* occupies an important position among the five principal deities. The antiquity of *Devī* or mother goddess is greater than that of any other deity, and her worship was prevalent in one or the other form in various parts of world right from prehistoric time, However the antiquity of female worship in India may be traced to the peasant culture of Balutistan.[17] But more definite proof of mother goddess worship has come from the terracotta figures finding from Harappan sites.[18] *Śakti* cult is one of the dominated cults of the area. *Devī* is worshiped in every village and her blessings are sought on every auspicious occasion and a goat is sacrificed as a protection against any evil. *Devī* is worshiped as *Kali*, *Jagga*, *Siṁhavāhinī Durgā*, *Pārvati* and *Mahishāsuramardini*. In the first two forms she is represented anicongraphically. In these forms her presence is represented by the high banner (*dhvaja*) installed on a raised stone platform or by a placement of a large white stone on the rock for the protection of society from any danger. The other forms in which she is worshipped are anthropomorphic.

Siṁhavāhinī Durgā: This form of goddess is worshipped under the common name of *durgā* however her sculptures in this aspect are only few in number. A stone sculpture of *Siṁhavāhinī durgā* from Hatkoti is now in the collection of State Museum Shimla and is displayed in Himachal State Museum (Pl.19). The fourhanded Goddess is seated enface in *lalitasana* on lion resting on its paws. The lion is shown in a state of relaxation indicating that the ferocious energy of the Goddess is not dormant. The Goddess has *kumbandha* and *blenduchur* on her head. The ancient text says that the face should not be round but broad like full moon as one finds in this image. The eyebrow is taut and arched like a full drawn bow. The neck has a beautiful trivet mark. The smooth plasticity of the figure appears in contrast to the sharply edged straight trident. The deity holds a *chasakpatra* in her lower right hand and trident in upper right hand while she holds a '*darpaṇ*' [19] in the upper left hand and *Bijpuraka* i.e. the seed of entire cosmos in lower left hand. A very thin ṣkirt held by a girdle similar to that of the Gupta period is worn at the waist. The plasticity of the image is smooth and buxom. The sculpture can be assigned to circa 8th century A.D.

Pārvati: Pārvati is worshiped as a consort of Śiva and its sculptures are very rare however she is found in association with Śiva in the other form of *Umā Maheśvara*. A stone sculpture of goddess *Pārvati* at Bachhoonch is shown standing on a lotus pedestal in *samabhaṅga* posture(Pl.19). She is wearing *jaṭāmukuṭa*, earrings, *hara, kankana, keyūra, angada, kaṭisūtra* and a fine sari, She is holding a *kamaṇḍalu* in the front left and a bow in the back left hands. Besides, she holds *sruk* in the back right hand while the front right hand is held in varada mudrā. On the lower right side a deer and on the left side a couching lion is shown. On the back slab a seated Gaṇeśa is shown on the left and a Shivliṅga in the right in the low relief. The sculpture shows close affinity with the stone image of Pārvati from Jageshwar in Almora district.

Mahishāṣuramardini: There are several mythical stories about the incarnation of Devī in the form of *Mahishasurmardini*.[20] A number of sculptures depicting this theme have been found from various sites. Goddess is shown with two to ten arms. However in the wall painting of the Śakti Devī temple Chhatrari the goddess is shown with thirty-six arms. The *Mahishasura* is also represented in different form right from the simple buffalo to a demon with a full human body.

Four-armed Mahishāsuramardini: A stone sculpture of four-armed goddess from Bachoonch is shown with *Jatta-jutta, Kuṇḍalas, Kankana, Keyūra,* pendent and is wearing a sari. *Kayabandha* is worn in *pattika* style and tied in a looped knot. She plants her right foot on the head of demon in *pratyālīḍa* posture and thrust the trident with front right hand into the neck of the demon and lifts the demon by tail upward with front left hand (Pl.21). She is holding a sword and a bell in the back right and left hand. A plain two-rimed plain hello is also carved on the back slab. The stone image is analogous to the Lakshna Devī bronze image (7th century A.D.) of Bharmour and to the sculpture of *Mahishāsuramardini* (8th century AD.) Jagatsukh, Kullu, which is displayed in the Himachal state Museum, Shimla (Acc. No 74.209). In the four-armed images of Himachal Pradesh, lion is usually conspicuous by its absence. The attributes held in the hands of the Devī i.e. bell, *khadaga*, trident are common to the other four armed images of Himachal Pradesh except for the one stone image hailing from Dhogi(Una) 8th century A.D. where she is shown holding a shield instead of bell.

Another four-armed image of *Mahishāsuramardini* is carved on the *tri-ratha* pedestal and is shown in the act of killing demon *Mahishasura*. The goddess is shown standing in *pratyālīḍa* posture and piercing the trident into the body of the demon with the front right hand, dragging the demon by the hair with front left hand (Pl.22). Mahishasura is shown coming out of the severed head of the buffalo and trying to free from the clutches of the Devī. Ornament worn by the goddess are large *chakar kundal* (earrings) and *urahsutra* (the hara of single variety) forming a knot between the cleavage of the well developed breast and falling in the form of the loop with the nayak maṇi in the centre. The image however lacks the vitality and force required for such type of act. The image belongs to c.10th-11th century A.D.

Another image of the goddess is very interesting, as it show a further development in the iconographic form of deity by showing the personification of demon solely in human form (23). The dynamic approach to the plastic conception of the deity is clearly visible in this sculpture. She has four arms, possessing a sword in the back right hand, thrusting the trident at the back of the demon with front right hand, dragging the tail of demon with front left hand and carrying a *pasa* in the back left hand. She plants her right leg on the foot of the demon. Though the goddess is shown carrying out the act mechanically yet the representation of the demon in pure human form is interesting and rare in the plastic art of India. Iconographically image belongs to c.8th – 9th century A.D.

Another stone sculpture of goddess wearing a traditional dress of the area is carved in folk style. She is wearing striped upper garments known as *chapkan* held at the waist by a girdle known as *gachhi* in this region (Pl.24). The demon is shown in human form emerging with folded hands out of the severed head of the buffalo. The two-armed goddess jabs the demon with the trident held in her right hand while dragging him by the hair with her left hand. The mount lion is shown taking part in the fight and pouncing on the buffalo. The sculpture is tentatively dated to c.16th -17th century A.D.

Eight-armed Mahishāsuramardini: Another image of goddess with aggressive expression represents an eight-armed Mahishāsuramardini (Pl.25). The image is iconographically very interesting and carved in folk style. She is clasping the two demons Chaṇḍa and Muṇḍa by the hair who are shown on either side of her feet, and striking the buffalo with a human face with trident held in the middle right hand. The representation of the demon in this form is rare and interesting. The deity is holding shield, bow, arrow, *cakra* and a curved sword in her other hands. The goddess is adorned with local costumes and jewellery. Her mount lion is carved on the right corner of the pedestal. The image can be assigned to mid 16th –17th century A.D.

Ganesha: Ganesha, was originally a non-Aryan deity.[21] He rose to the status of the great god in late-Gupta period after admission into Brahmanical pantheon. The most popular deity at the present time in Hindu Pantheon has not been mentioned in the Rig-Veda.[22] Moreover, Ganapati mentioned in the earliest literature refer to Brihaspati[23] not to Ganesha. He is clearly mentioned first time in Baudhayana Dharmsutra[24] with Rudra and his consort. In the later-Gupta period he became the most popular gods of the Hindu pantheon and occupies the main position among the five principal Hindu gods. He is worshipped before the commencement of every important work considered good for life. He was the deity for creating obstacle in human action and was prayed for removing them. No worship, no rites commence without paying homage to him to remove all the obstacles from the path of success. The devotees worship him as '*Vighnesha*' (the lord of obstacles), *Mangaldata* (he giver of welfare and auspicious things)*Buddhividhata* (god of wisdom) *Siddhidata* (the bestower of success).

The genesis of Gaṇeśa may be traced in the Mahābhārata[25] where the ganas of Rudra are said to have had animal's faces. The Matsya Purāṇa also records that Rudra ganas are *vyaghra-mukha* and gaja-mukha. Coomaraswamy traces the evolution of Gaṇeśa image from Gagna-yakṣamūrti from the Amravati railing.[26] Here elephantine faced yakṣa is crouching under the weight of a long serpent shaped garland held by other gana.[27] Another relief of Kushana period from Mathura depict five elephant-headed gana resembling Amravati figure.[28] Another representation of this type is found on the frieze of the stupa belonging to early centuries near Mihintale in Cylone,[29] in which one gana is represented with one tusk and elephant head. Paranavitance is of the opinion that the image may be a proto type of the classical Ganesha. In the early Gupta period we notice a further development of this type but its affinity to the yakṣa form still persists. A terracotta plaque from Bhiṭṭargaon brick temple belonging to early-Gupta period shows a four-armed figure in flying posture and his trunk touching the pot of sweetmeat placed in his right hand. It shows further development in iconographic form in Bhumra temple[30] figure where the he is shown seated on a raised seat wearing a bell necklace (ghantika mala). But in the later Gupta period Gaṇeśa makes its independent status and become one of the most popular deities of Hindu pantheon. Gaṇeśa became popular throughout India and even certain other region adjoining to the country.[31] Himachal Pradesh too, has, had quite a large share of the idols of the god. Stylistic and iconographic features of these stone sculptures are discussed below.

The earliest known sculpture of Gaṇeśa in Himachal dates back to the early seventh century A.D. now in state museum Shimla (Acc. No. 83.148). It was found at village Dohgi, Una district. It retains some features of Gupta sculpture. The sculpture appears quite powerful and somewhat bulky. The partly eroded image shows the deity seated in *ardha-paryankāsana*. His association with this sort of asana is because of his potbelly.

A stone sculpture of four-armed Ganesha[32] is placed in the niche of the **Durgā temple** at Hatkoti (Pl.26). The deity is seated on a double petaled lotus (vishva-padam) in the *ardha paryaṅka*. The backhands of the deity are raised up to the shoulder level (*urdhav-bahu*) and hold a *mulkanda*(radish)and a lotus of Gandharan type perhaps indicating the lingering influence from the northwest which is noticed only in the Pabbar and Ravi valley of Kullu. A *parśu*(battle-axe) heading downward with its tip placed on the pedestal is held in the right hand, which is a rare representation. The lower left hand of the deity is seen resting on the thigh (janu-vinyasta). The modelling is smooth, natural and proportions are classical. The sculpture seems to be of circa 9th century A.D.

A four-armed Gaṇeśa sculpture at Bachoonch is carved with typical Pratihara modelling showing local elements in the form of a lotus and long receptacle for *modak-patra*. Gaṇeśa is seated on a raised seat in *lalitasna* wearing ornamented conical crown, bell necklace (*kshudra-ghantika*) and *Sarpa-yajñopavīta*. The use of garland of bells is seen in *yakṣa* figures of early 2nd century A.D. These figures are the ancient prototype of the idols of the Ganesha. The god is represented as broad-shouldered, pot-bellied and has small-legs. The deity is as usual with one tusk, (*ek-danta*) large ears (*surpakarna)*, and elephantine face with plane halo at the back. The deity has four hands and his proboscis turned to the left is rising up to the shoulders. He holds a *parśu* (battle-axe) in his upper right hand and his lower right-hand held in *tarjan*i pose holds a rosary. His upper left hand holds a lotus while the lower left hand rests on his thigh and is holding the long receptacle of ambrosia-pot, touched by the proboscis(Pl.27). The image corresponds to the description of the *Aparajitaprichchha* and the *Agni-Purāṇa*. The sculpture may be assigned to early 10th century A.D.

A stone slab showing a four-armed Gaṇeśa seated in a variation of *ardha paryaṅka* on a *panch-ratha* pedestal is noticed at Bachoonch (Pl.28). The sitting arrangement of the deity is peculiar for the toes of his left foot are touching the ground while the right foot is lifted and faces the viewer, a posture which is usually adopted by the dancers in *chaturasara mudrā*. The deity holds the conventional emblems in his four hands and is scanty clad as well as bereft of any ornamentation. The image is interesting for it shows also the mount of the deity, a tiny rat held playfully by its tail in the right natural hand. Gaṇeśa is shown with extended ears (*surpakarna*) and his trunk is turned towards the right instead of left towards the sweet ball, which is held in the left hand. Though the image is of medieval period and its details are weathered nevertheless the image is interesting because of the peculiar iconographical traits.

A stone sculpture of dancing Gaṇeśa at Durgā temple Hatkoti is placed in a niche of the platform (Pl.29). This rare sculpture is artistically raising his right leg in the air (*bhujang-trasita*) while left leg slightly bent at brhamsthana in rhythmic pose. He wears a small a crown, a necklace, a bracelet, a *Sarpa-yajñopavīta* and a loincloth. He is shown, as usual, pot-bellied and has single tusk with proboscis turned to left. According to V.C. Ohri the feeling of heaviness is present in this image because the torso in this figure appears disproportionate. However this is not so, Gaṇeśa being the lord of Gana is often shown with distended belly '*lambodra*' and with stumpy legs' *khara vaktra pada*'. The deity has eight arms holding a snake above his head in the two backhands in whirling posture. The upper right hand is held in *tarjani mudrā* carries *aksutra* (rosary), middle holds a lotus and the lower hand holds a *parśhu.* He holds a *mulkanda*(radish) in the upper and *modakpatra* in lower right hand while the middle hand is broken. Two attendants holding patras are stand on either sides of the pedestal and two *gandharva* figures are shown in the relief on the upper portion of the back slab indicating the celestial region. The figure is full of grace and the artist has rendered all the details in a remarkable manner that such an apparently grotesque icon of this type is converted into and elegant piece of sculpture. On stylistic ground, this sculpture may be assigned to c. 10th century A.D.

Another sculpture of four-armed deity represented him seated in *lalitasna* on a lotus cushion. He is wearing a conical crown and bell necklace. The deity is shown as usual with elephantine face, fan like ears and a capacious belly. The snake head visible on the belly indicates that it served as *sarpa-yajñopavīta.* He is holding *savdanta* in right upper hand and lower hand is held in *abhya mudrā* while his left upper hands holds a lotus and a *modka-patra* with sweet balls arranged in heap and proboscis lotus and a *modka-patra* with sweet balls arranged in heap and proboscis placed high on it. In this image hands are raised invariably higher than the normal position.

Another sculpture of four-armed deity shows him seated in *lalitasna* on a lotus cushion. He is wearing a conical crown and a bell necklace. The snakehead visible on the belly indicates that it serve *as sarpa- yajñopavīta.* He is holding *savdanta* in right upper hand and lower hand is held in *abhya mudrā*.

Pandva Sculptures: The other unique finding of the valley is Pandava sculptures. The sculptures of Pandvas with Dropadi are under worship in a temple at Masli village on the left bank of Pabbar about 15 Km from Rohru.[33] The masculine figure of five Pandva with their wife Draupadi are placed on a concrete pedestal against the wall (Pl.30). These sculptures are carved in hard stone and are arranged in a similar manner as noticed in Deogarh relief of Gupta period. The central personage is apparently Yudhishthira, the two to his left are Bhima and Arjuna and those to his right, Nakula and Sehdeva. Draupadi the common wife of the five Pandvas is assigned the left corner at the last. According to Zimmer " these Pandva are regarded as themselves incarnation. Yudhishthra is a human manifestation of Dharma, the sacred Order of Life, Bhima represents the Wind God, Vayu; he is characterised by the huge iron club with which he smashed (by a foul) the thigh of the leading hero of the opponents, whom he had engaged in single combat. Arjuna is a human counterpart of Indra. Nakula and Sehdeva incarnate the twin 'Horseman God' The Ashvin. Draupadi, finally, is a duplicate of Indrani, the queen of the gods and spouse of Indra".[34] The seating posture, the moustaches, hairstyles and facial expression reminds the Kushana ethnic features. It is a common belief of people that Pandvas had spent some time in this place. There are many festival and folktales associated with the Pandva. There are some clans of Rajput i.e. Sathi and Panshi who believed to be the descendent of either the legendry Pandva and Kauruvas or of their followers and disciples. These sculptures on the stylistic features seem to be of c.15-16th century A.D.

Nakula: He is seated in *Sukhasna* and has rigid frontal pose. He is dressed in dhoti; a helmet and dagger sheath is also tucked in the girdle. He is wearing earrings and amulet is also seen on his neck. The locks of hair fall on both the shoulders. Urna is noticed between the eyebrows and a stencilled halo is carved behind the head. He is holding an *amrita-ghata* in left hand and a dagger like object in his right hand, which is resting on the left leg.

Sehdeva: He is seating in *Sopasaryanasna* and remaining features are same as in Nakula. A plane halo is carved behind the head and a dagger is tucked in the girdle. He is holding an *amrita-ghata* in his left hand and the right hand is resting on the knee.

Yudhishtra: He is seating in *Sopasaryana* and bears same features as noticed in the younger brothers. A sword is tide on the waist by a girdle.

Bhima: Bhima, the mighty warrior, is seated in *Paryankalitasana*. He is known for his great strength and brute courage, and for this reason he is installed as one of the guardian deities of the Hindu temples with Hanumāna, both sons of *Vayu*, the wind. He combines his vast strength with an irascible temper making him vindictive and cruel; 'terrible' as his name implies. He is holding a *Musla* (club) in his left hand and *amrita–ghata* in right hand. A Dagger is also seen on the waist. The rest of features are same as noticed above.

Arjuna: He is seated in *Paryankalitasana*. He has broad and massive shoulders, wears dhoti, a helmet, a long two-string Rudraksha beads *mala* and *Kuṇḍalas* are also seen hanging over the shoulders. Urna mark is noticed between the eyebrows and a lined halo is carved behind his head. His locks of hairs also cascade on the shoulders. He is holding bow in left hand and *amrita–ghata* in the right hand.

Dropadi: She is seated in *parynkasna* with both hands resting on her legs and holding an *amrita-ghata*. She is wearing long earring, a broad necklace and helmet. She is adorned with long and beautiful wig-shaped curls(churna-kuntala) falling on her back. A necklace hangs rhythmically above her full breasts. The body is sensitively modelled particularly the eyes, nose and chin. Her form recalls the ideal of a sophisticated female figure.

METAL IMAGES

The Pabbar valley harbours great treasures of metal images, a few which can be characterised as classical while others though in folk style have nevertheless great artistic and sculptural excellence. These images were generally made for temples and most of them are small in size except for one image of Mahishāsuramardini, which is about two meters in height and enshrined in the Durga temple as principal deity. The metal art of the Pabbar valley is influenced directly and indirectly by different art styles which flourished in the adjoining regions. No metal statuary earlier to Gupta period has been found in Himachal Pradesh. The Fatehpur Buddha from Kangra, which is now in the Lahore museum, is considered to be the earliest finding in this region dating back to early sixth century.[35] Dr. Coomaraswamy considered it as one of the fine specimen of the Gupta period. There must have been abundant production of bronzes in the Gupta period, but only a few preserved specimens are extant. It was in the Gupta period that the gestures were standardised and poses of religion statuary became codified on priestly order. After the decline of Gupta dynasty the northern part of India came under Harsha who encouraged the art of metal statuary and casting resulting in large number of metal images commissioned for temples and house worship. Famous Chinese traveller Hiuen Tsang mentions that he had brought back with him many statues of Buddha thus attesting to the practice of the metal craft during the reign of Harsha. The brass images of *Lakshna Devī, Śakti Devī, Gaṇeśa*and *Nandī* of Chamba are the excellent examples of the metal art that flourished in this region under the great ruler Harshavardhan.[36] The Pratiharas who extended their power in northern part after the death of Harsha also patronised the art activity consequently large numbers of temples and sculpture came up in this part. The metal image of Hari Rai at Chamba and Mahishāsuramardini at Hatkoti and *Kamakya Devī*[37] at Kamkhya temple at Karsog are considered to be the finest specimens of the Pratihara sculptures. The metal sculptures of Chamba shows close affinity with the Kashmir style while the sculptures of Pabbar valley follow closely the Pratihara style because of geographically, economically, and politically related closely to these areas. Such influences and infiltration were the consequence of political events and circumstantial trade route.

The image of the principal deity in Durgā temple at Hatkoti is of *ashtadhatu*. It depicts the goddess *Mahishāsuramardini*. It is considered to be one of the finest specimens of Pratihara period. Her one-foot rests on her vehicle-the lion while the other is placed on the snout of the demon as usually noticed. She is shown in the act of killing the demon *Mahishasur* with trident. Goddess has eight arms and holds the conventional emblems peculiar to this region i.e. Shield bell, bow, arrow *chakra, khadaga* and trident and with the lower most left hand is engaged in clutching tiny demon by the hair. The disc occurs twice in the image, first it is held in the hands of the Devī in *paryoga mudrā* and then it is seen half embedded in the belly of the buffalo demon (Pl.31). This action of the Devī where the chakra is used in the battle is analogues to the Mahishāsuramardini image of Bengal and Khajuraho 10th –11th century A.D.[38] The image of the deity or what one can make out of it shows a serene and a contemplative face with a flicker of smile playing on the gentle lips. The taut arched eyebrows the beaked nose and the double chin are the traits peculiar to the Pratihara period. The prabhavali at the back is coeval with the main image and contains an inscription in Sidhmatrika script and read as '*Bhatta sri sthanen kalpitam,*

Kayastha—left Dahila putra Padamnabha Raghvan Vardhitya ghatitam-right'.[39] The word kayastha[40] here is meant for Governor and the inscription reveals that this image is installed in Bhatta (pandit) place by the Governor, (name illegible) and cast by sculptor Padamnabha Raghvana son of Dahilla. On palaeographic grounds, epigraphists ascribe it to the 10th century A.D.

The two-meter high, ornamented *toraṇa* following nāgara form is of extra-ordinary iconographic interest. The present toraṇa is an amalgam of two important elements—the *sirachakra* and the *prabhavali*. The *sirachakra* of the sculpture is considered to correspond to *prabhamandal* or the halo of light which is supposed to surround all divine beings, in other words it is intended to serve a material representation symbolised by a circle of light shining around the heads of the gods. During the medieval period different type of *sirachakras* were adopted to decorate the figures, the commonest and the most popular of them was the shape of the lotus flower in full blossom placed just behind the head of deity as noticed in this image too. While the *prabhamandala* acts as a halo of radiant light, the *prabhavali* of the image is suppose to surround the whole person of the god and here in this image too is represented epileptically with several jwalas or protruding tongues of flames, though only in the upper half. Often special emblems of gods to whom the prabhavali belongs are sculptured on each side of it.

In the North-west India during the period of the Gurjara Pratiharas, the *prabhavali* was a common feature of the Vishṇu images depicting *dasavatara* scenes as noticed in the several images of Chamba, Mandi and Kullu. Here, we find two images of Dancing Gaṇeśa on either side and Śiva as *Vinadhara* seated on the pinnacle of the *prabhavali*. The depiction of the figures shows the influence of Shaivism in the Hatkoti region.

Cast in cine perdu(lost wax process) the *toraṇa* comprises of two parts, because of the massive size. The base of the *pitha* is plain –without any mouldings except for the *snanadroni*, which is oriented to the right. The *prabhavali* rests on two straight columns on either side and comprise of three *shakahas*. The central *shakha* or the band is treated as *bhadra shakha* and is flanked by *bhayashaka* slightly receding or meant to be treated so. At the base of the central *shakha* on each side the figures of Ganga and Yamuna standing on their respective vehicles and holding conventional emblems. The figures are adorned with flaming *prabhavalis* and wear streamers and *dhoti* of wet garment type of the Gupta period and are held at the waist with a girdle decorated with festoon of pearl strings from where tiny bells (*kushudra –ghantika*) are suspended. The bhadra *shakha* rising above the Ganga and the Yamuna figures are divided square panels filled in with four petalled lotus rosettes. The column terminates in to *tranga* brackets on which rests the weight of the superstructures of the aureole *prabhavali*. The *bhayashakha* shows in ascending order the motifs of *mangal gahata, bharvahaka*, elephant and a *varala* in separate panels. The *purnaghata* engraved at the base shows a narrow mouth a broad rounded belly and constricted decorated neck and four stylised petal are seen emerging from it. The *kichak* or the dwarf, the descendents of ancient *yakṣas* represented in the early Indian art of Barhut and Sanchi are here too shown with a potbelly and with the legs of the children and are seen lifting the weight with both the hands raised upwards. As seen in the classical art of India the elephant here too is rendered in his real form (pratikriti). Though slightly shown in striding position, his four legs are stationary. The gait of the elephant in Hindu literature is considered to be majestic and full of beauty (gajgamini). Being earth bound and heavy they are usually represented at the base to emphasize their mundane aspect in the cosmic world. Here the elephant is represented as domesticated and wears a velvet circular cushion on its back, which is tied around its belly with a rope. Above the elephant in a separate panel stands the *Simha varala* standing on his hind legs while the other legs are resting on the end of the scroll work issuing from his naval which shows the artistic innovation of the *shilpins*. The broad thigh of varala is marked with swirls or *urna* known as '*maramstha'l*. The face of the *varalu* is highly stylised and is that of a lion with a ram's horn. Its one paw is held in front of the chest and the other thrown forward as if it were ready to pounce upon (udyata).

The transverse beam or the cross bar as stated earlier is treated as *pithas* with recessions and offsets for the support of the miniature temples above which are harbouring dancing Ganesha. The terminals of the crossbeam are represented with makra heads above. The makara is given the shape made by art and has a raised snout (sund) of the elephant, sharp fangs of lion and with glaring eyes the makara looking at the warrior flying across in front of him with one leg tucked and the other thrown back in *halasna*; with the sword drawn warrior is ready to smite the monsters proboscis. The miniature temples on both side and one at the pinnacle are models of clarity and show in detail the various architectural members of the nagara temples. The *jaṅghās* in these miniature temples are treated in the form of *stambhas* and terminate with the band of recessed *kapotali* from whence arises the curvilinear spire marked with *bhūmis* and *amalkas* and topped by *chandrika* and *kalsha* finials. The fringe of the aureole is decorated with a row of divinities framed with in halos.

There are few other images, which are miniature in size but depict the principle deities of Hindu pantheon and are under worship at Hatkoti and other temples. The establishment of Islamic rule in the North India, resulted into the disintegration of the metal art. The Northern India, which became the battlefield for many foreign invaders, resulted in the destruction of religious institutions and temples and most of the sculptures were smashed and melted. The cultural link of the valley was disconnected and thereafter, local need for cult icons could only be satisfied by local crafters which resulted in misunderstood iconography and deviation from the classical prototypes thus producing local style of their own which progressed into folk bronzes. The output of such an art represents a unique complex of primitive impulses and traditional practices both subjected to sophisticated influences and to highly local developments; aside from aesthetic consideration. The specimens of this interesting metal art can be noticed at various temples in the valley and mainly represented by the idols of Mahishāsuramardini and Ganesha. There is large number of Mahishāsuramardini idols at the Hatkoti complex and two such images are also in the Mahasu temple Badiar, devta

Banar and other temples of the valley. Masks are the other type of metal craft found in the valley. These are particularly used for worship in the temple and represent a specific deity. The mask mainly represents the local Devī or the Devta. These masks are placed in the sanctum and are carried out in a palanquin (rath) of the devta during the festive occasion.

MEMORIAL STONES

The practice of erecting memorial stones in commemoration of the deceased is very ancient.[41] The erection of memorial stones was also prevalent in the Pabbar valley. These memorial stones are very simple, without any inscriptions and are usually in the form of small slab of slate or stone on which the figure of the deceased is rigidly carved in comparison with the memorial stones of Mandi and the fountain stone slabs of Chamba where these are of a more elaborate character, and adorned with ornamental carvings and numerous figures. The tradition of erecting memorials in the commemoration of departed soul is still prevalent in the area. When a person of an upper caste dies, the relatives of the deceased install a *parnala* (water tap) at the source of water and use to carve the name and date of death on a slab. However, it was regarded as a royal privilege in the eastern part of the state (i.e. Mandi, Kullu and Suket) and there it was customary among the royal lineage (Raja and Rana),[42] however, there were no such restrictions in this region, as these were also erected in the memory of others also. The tradition of erecting memorial stone which was common in the Rajputana and Saurashtra region possibly came to these parts with the migration of people.[43] It is commonly observed from the *vamsavalis* that most of the ruling families of the region draw their pedigree from the powerful Rajput families of central India.[44] It is a well established fact that when the Muslim stress on Hindus increased in the plains these people migrated to the hilly region for safety and purity of blood.[45] In this way the tradition of memorial stone came into existence in these parts and became common among these families because there is no memorial stone noted so far in Himachal before the 10th century A.D.[46] Such type of memorial stones are known as *Barselas, Pitr, Paap, Manes, Naga, Varun Deva, Panihar, Naun,* etc in the different parts of the state. These memorial stones are commonly found near the source of water one can notice the large number of such *parnalas* inscribed with the name and the year of death of the person and there was a common belief among the people that by erecting the memorial stone near the source of water, the soul of the deceased find peace in the eternal world. The idea underlying to place the memorial stones near the source of water appears to be two fold. In the first place when the tablet is merely attached to cistern or well the disembodied spirit seems to acquire merit from the act of charity performed by the dead man's descendent. Secondly there is a common belief among the people that by erecting the memorial stone near the source of water the spirit will be able to quench its thirst whenever it wishes.

There is also a custom to keep the memorials in the houses to commemorate the deceased and are always made of metal either silver or gold which is known as Paap. These Paaps were worshiped in every month on the special day i.e. *Sankranti.* By offering the special feast, the soul of the deceased person became happy and grants blessing for the success of every work and if it is not worshiped the departed soul becomes unhappy then it will create obstacle in the every field of life.

Many travelers and archaeologists have noticed memorial stones in different parts of Himachal. It was Capt. A.F. Harcourt who first brought to notice memorial stones of Naggar and mentioned them as 'a curious collection of what resembles tombstone'[47] Later on, J. Ph. Vogel, A. Cunningham, A. H. Franke and P. Chetwood identified these memorial stones with different names. Vogel termed these memorial stones as *mohras*[48] but his interpretation seems to be hastily drawn as *mohras* are associated with gods and goddesses and are used for worship in the temples. Franke called them *Sati-Stones*[49], because of the large number of female figures.

Usually three types of memorial stones are found in the valley (1) Royal person Stones (2) Hero-stones (3) Sati-stones. The memorial stones of the first type were erected in the commemoration of the royal person lest their glory, splendor and the prowess be forgotten by the public. The second type of memorial stones was erected in the memory of the persons who sacrificed their lives in the battlefield for the sake of their motherland or other brave deeds concerning the welfare of the society. The society in turn recognized their sacrifices and valiant services and admired their courage as well as contribution. Third type of memorial stones was erected in the memory of sati who ascended the funeral pyre of their deceased husband. The sati stones are found only in a small number because it was considered to be the prerogative of the women of royal families who as widowhood was the social stigma for them and remarriage was also not accepted in this section. The rite of sati was even performed by immolating widows of the deceased forcibly so that high character of the family may not be tarnished. It was only a few women in the other section of the society who performed the rite of Sati with their husband in the wake of dedicated love and also to save their sanctity. Otherwise remarriage was always accepted in this society in general and here the widowhood was not the social stigma. They enjoyed all respects in the new family and their status in the society remained as respectful as it was before. The stories of *Sati* immolating themselves on the funeral pyre are still alive in the folklore of the region.

In some memorial stones, the deceased person is shown seated on a couch and smoking a *huqqa*. The depiction of *huqqa* signifies the royal status of the deceased. Besides, his wife is shown holding a water jar in her hands, which is considered necessary in the ritual of sati. A rectangular block of stone showing the royal person seated cross-legged on couch at Badyar in a bawari. A female holding *huqqua* in her hand and is offering it to seated person signifying the royalty of the deceased person.

In hero stones, the hero is shown lashed with weapons, riding on a horse the deceased person indicating that this brave person has sacrificed his life in the battle field. A memorial stone lying on the near the Hatkoti village depicts the hero seated on the horse and lased with arms in the upper panel while in the lower panel he is shown holding the hand of his devoted wife who immolated herself in the funeral pyre (Pl.32). In the memorial stones of other part of Himachal the horse riders invariably appear in the lower panel.

In Sati-stones, the carving generally low relief almost like linear sketches and the women are shown with up-raised hands (Pl.33). The memorial stones erected in the memory of these deceased people could be noticed at several parts of the valley.

A memorial stone slab placed outside Durgā temple at Hatkoti showing females standing in the rows holding the right hands of each other and upraising their left hands, symbolizing that they were leaving the world to accompany with their husband in the other world.[50] This stone is the imitation of wooden block which was ruined some time 35-40 years ago. Tradition of keeping many wives was very common in the valley and number of wives indicated the symbol of royalty in the society.

In another stone slab, a female wearing a striped skirt lashed with the weapons and a pot of sacrificial water is lying on her right side. The slab is indicating that this brave woman had sacrificed her life in the battlefield for the sake of her motherland.

Reference:

1. Aggarwal, V.S., *Evolution of the Hindu Temple, Indian Civilisation Series*, V.
2. Munshi, K.M., *'The Saga of Indian Sculptures*, A. Goswamy (ed) Indian temple sculptures, p.4.
3. Ohri, V.C., (ed), *Art and Archaeology of Himachal Pradesh*, Some aspects, Himachal State Museum, p.36.
4. Marshall, J., Mohen-jo-dara and the Indus civilization, I, pp.52-6, Pl. XII, 17. M.S. Vats, Excavation at Harappa, I, pp.129-30, Pl. CXIII, Pl. 303.

5. (III 2.16,19).
6. Krishna, Brajesh., The Art under Gurjara-Pratihara, p.192 foot note.
7. Shastri, A.M., *Symbols on Tribal Coins.* ' An Interpretative Study'. Seminar paper on the Tribal coins of Ancient India. J.P. Singh and Nisar Ahmed (ed), p.89.
8. Chauhan, Hari, Sculptures of Pabbar Valley- *A Journal of Oriental Institute,* M.S. University, Baroda, Vol.50, 2000. (Golden Jubilee Issue).
9. Coomaraswamy, A., *The Dance of Shiva.*
10. Iyer, K. B., *Indian Art*, p.36.
11. Chauhan, Hari, Sculptures of Pabbar Valley- A Journal of Oriental Institute, M.S. University, Baroda, Vol.50, 2000. (Golden Jubilee Issue).
12. Rao, T.A.G., *Elements of Hindu Iconography*, Vol. I, Introduction p.20.
13. Banerjea, J.N., Development of Hindu Iconography, p.261, plate XXIV.
14. Pandey, L.P., *Sun worship in Ancient India*, pp.1 ff.
15. Krishna, Brajesh., *The Art under Gurjara-Pratihara*, p.155.
16. Chauhan, Hari, Sculptures of Pabbar Valley- *A Journal of Oriental Institute*, M.S. University, Baroda, Vol.50, 2000. (Golden Jubilee Issue).
17. Piggott, Stuart., *Pre historic India*, p.127.
18. Mackay, E., *Early Indus Civilization*, pp. 53-54.
19. Ohri, V.C., in *Arts of Himachal* refers to Darpan as shield and Laxman Thakur is of the same view. However see catalogue of Stone sculptures in the Museums of H.P. p.35 S.M. Sethi identified this attribute as

'Darpan' . According to him the attribute is facing the devi rather than the enemy.

20. Singh, Seo Bahadur., *Brahmanical Icons in Northern India*, p.157.
21. Sampurnand, *Hindu Deva Parivara Ka Vikas*, p.147.
22. The reference to Brahmanaspati in Rigveda (II,23,1) and the Atharvaveda (VII,31,1), as the lord of all Brahma-Yakshas, Ganapati and the supreme king Jyeshtharaja, does not mean for Ganesha.
23. Aitareya-Brahmana (I,21(Hag p.15), Śuklayajurveda (Madhyandiniya Samhita, XXII.
24. II, 5,6.
25. IX, 45, 75ff.
26. Coomaraswamy, A., *Yaksha*, I, p.7.
27. Ibid, Pl, 23, Pl. 1.
28. Aggarwal, V.S., Studies in Indian Art, p.189.
29. Getty, op. cit, p.25 Pl. XXII (e).
30. Banerjee, R.D., op.cit., Pl.XV, a.b.
31. See Ganesha by Getty.
32. Chauhan, Hari., Hatkoti a place of religious sanctity, *Marg Magzine*, vol.53, No.3, p.60.
33. Handa, O.C., *Temple Architecture of the Western Himalaya*, Wooden temple, p.171.
34. Zimmer, Heinrich., *Myths and Symbols in Indian Art and Civilization*, p.62, footnote .
35. Vogel, J.Ph., Inscribed Brass statue from Fathepur (AR ASI 1904-05) pp.107ff.

36. Goetz, Hermann., *Studies in the History and Art of Kashmir and the Himalayap.* p.139.
37. Aryan, Subhashni., *Marg Magazine.*
38. Nagar, Shanti Lal., *Mahishasurmardini in Indian Art*, Pl.38, 41.
39. Himachal State Museum, *Himachal Art and Archaeology, Some aspects*, Shimla,1980, p.34.
40. Trivedi, Sudhir Kumar., *Madhya Bharat ki Pratiharkalin kala aivam Sthapatya,* p.22.
41. Rig-Veda X.18.3, Satapatha Br. XIII.8.1.,29.1.2 , Ancient India, No.2, pp.9ff.
42. Hutchinson, J., & Ph. Vogel, *History of Punjab Hill State*. Reprint, 2000, p 381.
43. Grierson, George A., *Linguistic Survey of India*, p.14.
44. Mandi and Suket rulers from Sen dynasty, Kullu from Pal and Chamba ruler from Varman dynasty.
45. Hodgson- *The language, Literature and Religion of Nepal*, part II p.37.
46. In Chamba the inscribed memorial stones of 10th century are noticed.
47. Harcourt, A.F.P., *Himalayan District of Kullu, Lahaul and Spiti.* P.108.
48. Vogel, J. Ph., A.S.I. Annual Report 1902-3, p. 215.
49. Franke, A.H., *Antiquities of Indian Tibet*, pl.1, p. 9.
50. Jain, Madhu., *The Abode of Mahashiva*, Pl.28 identifies this memorial slab as Sapta-matrika panel, but here the females are raised their hand in vam- posture and such type of posture is peculiar to the sati stone only.

CHAPTER 5

FAIRS AND FESTIVALS

Fairs and festivals are an important part of the cultural life of the people and play an important role in the socio-religious fabric of the society. Generally the fairs are held at a time when the people are free from their harvest engagements. The festivals are celebrated for relaxing tiredness and paying obedience to the local deity for good production. Every region has their own village deity and festivals are celebrated in his honour. Some festivals are also held for the peace and prosperity of the area. *Bishnu, Jagra, Tana, Ashtmi, Jatar, Bhoj, Bhunda* and *Shant* are among the most popular celebrations in the valley. In these festivals the local deity comes out from the temple and blesses his devotee.

Shant: It is one of the rare celebrations of the area and is celebrated after the gap of 12 years and even much more gaps because it is very expensive festival and requires large quantity of food grains and goats. This festival is celebrated for the peace and prosperity of the area. The village deity warns its public that some calamities and evils may happen in the area and advices to organize this celebration so that area could be saved from such heavenly csurse. Then villagers start making necessary arrangements for this celebration. The host deity invites the surrounding gods and godlings. A *Mahayajna* starts at the temple of village deity and continue seven days and at the last day the invited deities come with its public (*khund*) in a procession lased with weapons and make the dance in the ground (Pl.34). On the next early morning these *devtas* take a round of the village and goats are sacrificed at a specific interval all around and final celebration takes place at the top of the temple. The priest accompanied by the *goors(*a man who passes oracle of the deity) of the deities climbs at the top of the roof of the temple and recites the hymn and goats and sheep's are sacrificed in the name of all evil spirits to ensure the peace and prosperity of the area.

Bhunda: Bhunda is the local term for the *bali* (offering) or a feast to the gods. The *bali* to the deity in the religious ceremony of this region may be in the form of animal, coconut, pumpkin or a cock. But in *bhunda yajna* a human being designated for this purpose as *jailly* is offered to the gods as a *bhunda*. Since offerings and sacrifices were made in mass scale in the festival it became popular as *bhunda yajna.*[1] It was especially common among agricultural people of this region who sought the guarantee of fertility of the soil. In this *yajna* victims were ritually sacrificed in a manner which was supposed to please or appease the gods as a payment for favourable intervention in an event of social importance or to forestall unfavourable events.

The practice of *narbali* can be traced back through the Brahmanas to Vedic period when human sacrifices were offered to Vedic deities to gain religious merit. The earliest reference of human sacrifice occurs in the first book of the Rig-Veda. It contains seven hymns supposed to have been recited by one Sunahsepa when he was bound to a stake (*yupa*) preparatory to being immolated. According to a story given in the Aitreya Brahmana of the Rig-Veda, King Harischandra had made a vow to sacrifice his first born to Varuna, if that deity would bless him with children. Consequently a child Rohita was born and Varuna accordingly claimed it, but under various pretexts Rohita ran to the forests and wandered there for six years while Varuna afflicted the father with dropsy. At last Rohita met a starving Brahman named Ajigarta who agreed to sell him his son Sunahsepa for hundred cows to be offered as a substitute.[2] There is also a reference of *narbali* in Shatpath Brahmin.[3]

Bhunda is the old *narmedi* jag held in Kullu and Shimla from very ancient times. The beginning of the fair is supposed to originate at Nirmand. The legend holds that *rishi* Jamadagni became angry for some reason with his wife Ambika and was slain by son Parsuram at the behest of his father. In expiation Parshu Ram gave lands in charity to the Brahmin of Nirmand who in return agreed to spend 1/10 of produce on this *bhunda* fair. It is also believed that the festival is celebrated to absolve Parshuram of the sin committed by him. The fair is held once in 12 years and completed in five days. But now it is celebrated after many years possibly because of expenditure involved. Apart from Nirmand this fair was also held at Nither, Baina, Dhansa, Dalash,Gorah and Manjeoti in Rampur and Pujarli, Dalgaon, Kulgaon, Nandla and Bachoonh in Rohru tehsil.

The ceremony in its original form consists of a long and thick rope of the diameter of about 2.5 inch, its one end secured to a peg embedded on the hill top while the other is fastened at the bottom of the slope and then letting a man slid down the rope on a wooden *kathi*(sleigh). The man of *beda* cast who performs this act is known as *'jailly' or beda. Beda* is a small community of the menial class found in Shimla hills and Garhwal[4], whose function is a sort of priestly type. When the deities fix the date of function through the oracle of their *goor* the selected man (*jailly*) is called on by the temple committee in the village and informed about the will of the deity. The devotees of the deity collect the *munj(grass)*, cut at a propitious time to the accompaniment of music, about one year before the fair and *Beda* himself prepare rope out of it, performing constant offering while working at it.[5] When it is made to the right length, it is placed in the temple and all efforts are made to maintain its sanctity. No one may approach it with shoes or cross over it and any one defiling the norms is fined with a goat, which is sacrificed, and the rope then must be re-made. It is revered and accorded the status of *devta. Havan-yajna* starts in the temple a week before the commencement of final ceremony and oblation are made into the *Havan -kund*(fire-pit) with the chant of mantras. The whole *yajna* is entrusted to the kali to seek her blessing for the peace, prosperity and safety of the area. The host deity invites the surrounding gods and god lings on the last day who arrive in a procession escorted by *Khund*[6] singing and dancing and brandishing swords with folk musical instrumentalists blowing their instruments at full pitch and the host village providing them feast from the *bhandar*(treasure). At day break the next early morning these *devtas* take a round of the village (pher)) and goats are sacrificed at the place of halt under the instruction of *goor* and final celebration takes place on the temple roof. The ceremony of *Shikha-pher* begins with priests accompanied by the *goor* and the members of temple committee climbing on the top of the temple roof. Here the local Brahmin recites the hymn (mantras) to invoke the mountain goddesses as well as to evil spirits and offering them *roate* (bread morsels), floor, goat etc. to appease them and ensure peace and prosperity. There is a belief that if these mountain spirits are not appeased they will interfere and disturb the peace and bring natural calamity in the region resulting in loss of life and damage to the crops of the area. On the fixed time the rope is carried on the shoulders reverently and taken to the cliff where it is fastened securely. On the appointed day, the *beda(jailly)* takes a bath and is taken to the *kund*. The Brahmin worships him, and accords him the status of god. He is then clothed in a white dress and endowed with turban (*pagri)* and *panchratans*(five valuable metal put in the mouth of a Hindu at the time of death) are placed in the *pagri*(turban) of the *beda* .He is then carried on the *rath* of host deity in a procession commencing from the temple to the place of actual ceremony in the company of folk musical orchestra while his wife, relatives and the huge gathering of the spectators remain at the lower end of the rope. At the signal by the priest, the rope of the pulley is cut and the *beda* slides down with horrifying speed. The *beda's* feet are immersed knee deep into the heavy sand bags tied to his legs to maintain balance while sliding down the slope. The *beda* thus slide down perching precariously on the wooden sleigh placed on the rope and a slight tilt in the balance will hurl him down hundreds of feet below. Such is the momentum that his body is swept backward and he throws his arms up fluttering red handkerchiefs in his hands while speeding down the slope(Pl.35). If he reaches safely at the bottom people rush and jostle with each other to snatch the *panchratan* tied on the turban of *beda* which is considered auspicious. Afraid of being trampled down by the mad rush to snatch the *panchratna* the *beda* hurriedly throws down the turban on the ground escaping from the crowd. Then he and his family is taken to the temple in the procession on the *palki* of the *deovta* where they are offered with money, cloth, jewellery and other things. After the ceremony is over the rope is brought back to the temple as the testimony to the celebration being over and one can notice many such ropes hanging in the temple.

There is no early reference or written document, which could throw a considerable light on the origin of the *yajna*. It is only the later records preserved in the temple narrating the customs, income and expenditure occurred in the festival. As stated earlier the fair seems to have originated from the site which is of archaeological importance yielding large number of monuments dating back to 8th -9th century A.D. If the legend connected with the celebration has some historical bearing than the possibility of its beginning can be traced back to a very early period. The festival is celebrated in Rampur and its surrounding areas which were once the part of Rampur State perhaps from where it spread to the other parts.

It was the European travellers and officials who later recorded the tradition of this fair and mentioned it in their accounts. According a folk-lore, a *beda* had met his death owing to the rope giving way in 1856 and in 1868 *beda* slide was banned by the then commissioner Col. Lek. A white goat was substituted for the human sacrifice in 1868. H. L.H. Shuttle worth had witnessed *bhunda-yajna* in March 1919 at Nirmand and presented a paper on 21st April 1922 at Dutch Oriental Society "An inscribed metal mask discovered on the occasion of the *bhunda* ceremony at Nirmand".[7] Captain A.F. Harcourt also gave a short account in the "Himalayan Districts of Kullu, Lahul & Spiti".[8] The other dates about the celebrations of festivals are 1885A.D. 1904, 1919, 1933, 1962, and 1981A.D. at Nirmand.

As stated earlier it is not necessary that the person who slides down the rope always meets his death. In 1819 William Moorcroft met in Garhwal one *banchu*(beda), who had slid down on 16 occasions in the festival without any hazard.[9] There is no other information on record except that in the year 1856 a *beda* named Sarbanu had met his death. A *beda* had narrow escape and landed safely at Kharan in June 1987 and at Dansa in 1990 respectively.

Bhunda-yajna was also celebrated in the Rohru region, the boundary of which intersects with the Rampur. Bhunda was held in December1991 at Nandla, in 1994 Dalgaon, in1984 at Kulgaon, in 1995 at Pujarli (near Summerkot) and after a gap of 70 years at Bachoonch in 23nd -26th December, 2005 and recently in Rampur at Deothi village on 12th December, 2006. The members of *beda* family who reside at Dalgaon take part in this ceremony. Beda Surat Ram slided down at Pujarli while his younger brother Kanwar Singh performed four times at other places without suffering any serious injury. However, now the length of the rope has decreased substantially from 500-600 meters to 100-200 meter to minimize the risk. The administration makes all necessary measures to protect the life of *beda* by putting nets below the ropes but hesitates to ban the ceremony as it may go against the religious sentiments of the people.

Bhoj: It is the festival of the *Koli* clan. The deity of this class asks them to celebrate this function. People start making necessary arrangement for this function and on the decided date the principal *devta* of the village is invited to take part and other local *devtas* of this class are also invited to take part in this celebration. The festival starts with seeking the blessing of the principal *devta* and other *devta* shows their tricks by passing iron rod through their lips, nose and chicks etc. and sheep and goats are sacrificed in the name of the *devtas* and feast is served as a *bhog* of the temple.

Jagra: The word '*jagra*' is derived from the Sanskrit word *jagarana* meaning to keep awake all night in devotion. This festival is held in the commemoration of Mahasu (Maha Shiva) in the month of *Bhadon* (September) on the fourth day of the bright phase of the moon. People from the surrounding villages gather around the temple. Huge bonfires are lit in the temple courtyard when darkness falls, the worshipers of the *devta*, with lighted torches in their hand dance and sings the sacred song (*Birsu*) in honour of *devta* for some time and make the round of brazier (*chira*) on which they later fling the blazing faggot(Pl.36). This is one of the major ceremonies enjoyed by the people and the sacred song (*Birsu*) is sung in honour of the *devta*. The misty mountain air fills with the rising sound of drum, trumpet, Kartal, Bells and the energy of the *devta*. On the next morning the sacred vessels are taken to the neighboring spring in a procession for bath, singing song in the honour of *devta*. After washing the sacred vessels and other sacred pots the procession come back to the temple and *devta* palanquin also dance with the devotee and after some time *devta* also hears the grievances of the devotees and passes the decisions through *goor*. After that the *devrath* is placed back in the temple where the main idol of the *devta* is bathed and *puja* is performed. The *Kardars*(temple committee members) stay in the temple and spend the whole night in the temple. In this way the ceremony takes place and function is closed after two days celebration.

Bishu: It is the fair of spring season, Baisakhi. It is held on the first *Baisakh* every year. Every person puts on his or her best and assembles in the temple complex of the village *devta*. The village deity is carried in a palanquin poised on the shoulder of two men. The musicians, known as *dhaki*, beating drums, kettledrums and blowing trumpets, precede the palanquin. The village deity dances with the devotees and palanquin start oscillating on the shoulders and devotees sing the songs in the honour of *devta.* In the bishu fair the sacred vessels and other things are also washed on the spring and same way as followed in the Jagra festival.

Ashtmi: Ashtmi is celebrated twice in a year in the month of *Baisakh* and *Bhadon.* It is celebrated in Durga temple complex at Hatkoti during the *Navratra.* The people flock from different parts of Himachal and other States to get the blessings of the *devi* during these auspicious days.

Reference:

1. European travelers correlate 'bhunda' with bhandar but this festival has no relation with bhandar .Bhandar is a sacred place where the treasure of the deity is kept.
2. Clayton, A.C., *The Rig-Veda and Vedic Religion*, p. 128.
3. Shatpata Brahmana 13 & 6-7.
4. Berreman, Gerald. D. Hindus of Himalyas, pp.67-68.
5. Sometimes the event of collecting grass starts about two-and half month before commencement of ceremony. It is also easy to provide the security of the rope and maintain its sanctity.
6. The martial branch of khasha.
7. Postel, M., A. Naven, K. Mankodi, *Antiquities of Himachal*, Bombay, Appendix-C, p.279-283.
8. Harcourt, A.F., *Himalayan Districts of Kullu, Lahul & Spiti*, New Delhi,1972, p.96-98.
9. Moorcroft, William, George Trebeck, *Travels in the Himalayan Provinces of Hindustan from 1819 to 1825*, London, 1841, Vol. I, p.17.

CHAPTER 6

WOOD CARVING

The term 'wood carving' implies the process in which wood is fashioned for aesthetic purpose. It is one of the very ancient craft of India. Wood is widely used for construction and embellishment of palaces, temples and houses, as it is easily available and readily tractable material. It was the most popular medium for the artisan to express their artistic skill from very early times. There is no doubt that woodcarvings in relation to architecture is of a very ancient origin although we have no surviving examples of the past work due to perishable nature of the material. But it can be safely assumed that even in very early ages, since the down of civilization wood was widely used for varied purposes. Woodcarvings find mention in Veda[1], Epics, Buddhist literature, as also in the account of the foreigner travelers[2] who have described the splendor of this art, the prototype of which one can still find in the cave temples of Maurya and early Gupta period[3].

Wood is not only used for the construction of buildings but also for their decoration. The carved doors and window-frames, balconies of temples, carved panels, brackets, pillars and houses present excellent specimen of woodcarvings. Besides, these architectural purposes, wood was also used for making images of divinities and semi divine being, which speak of the artisan's mastery over the technique of woodcarving. A good number of the examples of these woodcarvings could be noticed in the temples and the old houses. Ornately and beautifully carved wooden panels and sculptures testify to the height to which the craft had reached in the early days. The woods used for this work are deodar, pine, walnut, *shisham tun*, etc. The composition is greatly influenced by the grains of the timber used. Describing the special characteristic of wood which determines the quality of work to be done, Sir George Watt remarks: "The art conception seen in wood work have been greatly influenced by the grains of the timber employed, such as the deep undercutting and sculpture that is possible with teak, redwood and walnut, the low relief shisham and deodar, the incised designs of ebony, the intricate and minute details of sandal and the barbaric boldness of rohira, sal and babul and other course grained and hardwood".[4] For instances, the deep cutting is provided on the redwood and walnut, whereas the low relief carvings on pine and deodar.

Woodcarvings so far discovered are very interesting but the carving of artistic merit rarely goes beyond the 17th century A.D. The obvious reason for the absence of old examples are the perishable nature of the material. The earliest wood carving so far discovered in Himachal is from Bharmour in Chamba district. The façade, door frames, lintel, window frames and ceilings of Lakshna Devi temple at Bharmour and Shakti Devi temple at Chatarari is carved with the figures of divine, human, animal, floral and geometrical patterns in the classical style of post-Gupta period and belongs to early 8th century A.D., and other examples of carvings like that of other part of India rarely goes beyond the 17th century A.D. It is usually noticed that when the carving gets decayed it is replaced with the new carving. The other reason is that the wooden structure could not survive for a long period and were reconstructed several times. The woodcarvings of this region greatly impressed the European travellers who visited this region in 19th century and they did not forget to praise in their account the splendour of this unique and ancient art particularly in the field of constructive architecture and decorative art which was so popular with the people.

The craftsmen engaged in wood work is known as '*Bari*'(Mistri)and he works with his traditional technique. His tools are of simple character and of indigenous make, prepared by the local blacksmith. They are made to specification and under the instruction of the carver. The crafts man uses wide variety of tools ranging from few to hundred in numbers, according to the extent of artistic ability, the nature of carving and the quality of wood on which he works. The tools primarily used by the carvers are *aari* (hand-saw) *basola* (adze), *randa* (plane), *nehan* (chisel), *hathodi* (hammer), scale and drilling equipment, etc. The most important tools used by the carver for minute carving are chisels and gauges of various sizes and shapes ranging from the point of a needle to three-fourth of an inch. Every artisan has his own collection of a wide range and variety of theses carving instruments commensurate with his skill in his using.

The selection of wood is done with meticulous care, which helps the artisan to be at best in workmanship at his best. The piece of wood selected for carving is first cut off in required size and trimmed carefully with adze to give the desired shape. After drawing the outline, the superfluous portion is first taken out to give it a rough shape. The real technique and skill however lie in the subsequent operations, which require the true knowledge of the carver regarding the forms and correct use of the tools which would enable him to deftly take out the unwanted portion by means of gauges and chisels of different sizes with manipulation of strokes through the movement of hands. Starting with broad outlines, the artisan proceeds from simple to intricate carving.

The places best known for rich ornamentation, skilful execution and characteristic designs are Hatkoti[5], Jubbal, Bachoonch, Gawas, Summerkot, Badiyar, Pujarli and Rohru[6] area etc. In Hatkoti, the ceiling of Śiva temple[7] is richly carved. The figures of Gods and Goddesses are carved out of a block of wood measuring 2x2 feet and then made to fit into the ornamented wooden frame (Pl.37, 38). Woodcarvings have also been noticed at Durgā temple. The eve's planks of the temple are carved with the scenes depicting the life led by the deities during their various incarnations (Pl.39). The deities are also shown in combat with the demons in battlefields. The floral and geometrical patterns add to the beauty of the panels and make them beautiful and interesting. Vishnu with its various incarnations is carved beautifully showing the mastery of the contemporary artesian in wood. The motifs of interlacing snakes (the symbols of fertility)[8] also serve the part of woodcarving on the panel. In the temple, the carved hanging bells of wood produce the pleasing sound with the blowing of air. The *chabutra* in the temple complex stands as an ideal example of contemporary woodcarvings. It is richly carved with intricate floral and geometrical patterns.

The temple of Devta Banar at Pujarli has rich woodcarvings. The temple is fully embellished with floral and geometrical patterns. However, the battle scenes are also carved. The battle scenes are depicted either on the door or in the eaves of the frontal part of the temple. The eaves planks are also carved with the warriors marching to the battlefields on the beat of the musician's war drum. The floral and geometrical patterns add to the beauty of the temple and have their significance in *vastu* texts. The floral motifs are employed to ornament the various architectural features. The façade of the temples their columns and doorframes and other architectural members are adorned with the pattern of intertwined creepers and leaves. The stem of the creeper is shown curving, arching and curling. Along the side of the stem, leaves are represented with aesthetic grace.

The entrance door of Mahasu devta temple at Badiyar has very interesting woodcarvings. The doorjambs show the figure of minor deities on either side and their names-*Kaulu* and *Narsing* are carved below. The artisan has drawn this idea from the legend that these two deities are the gatekeepers of the Devta Mahasu. They are holding a spear in hands and are standing on the lotus pedestal. Through the employment of such a symbol, the architect attempt to indicate the power, majesty and potential of the god consecrated within. The *dwarpalas* are carved in as erect posture and carrying the weapon in their hands. The upper part is embellished with the floral patterns, while the lintel of the door is carved with the image of Gaṇeśa in the center along with his mount rat and the ends are carved with the lion's heads known as *simhamukh*. The horizontal beams of the frontal part of the temple are carved with interlacing snakes and floral patterns, adding to the beauty of the temple.

In addition to these places, there are also a large number of temples[9] in the valley but the motifs and style of these carvings are similar. In Sikroo temple at Rohru the symbols of Sun is depicted in large number in various forms. Sunflower, revolving charka and the floral and geometrical patterns are the most common symbols used for adornment of the temple. Many animals and birds have also been represented in a graceful and imaginative manner in the architectural members. The artist uses the lion motifs to characterize the royalty and the sovereignty of the temple. The interlacing snakes (naga pasha) are also carved on the architectural members. Similarly, the artist represents various animals and birds in a poetic and lyrical manner. Among the bird swan, peacock, pigeon and *monals* are also used to decorate the panels of the wood.

Wooden sculptures of a very high order are an integral part of the temples. The sculptural tradition has taken on the responsibility of expressing some of most profound ideals and experience of man through simple, easily understandable symbols, which have a direct bearing on everyday life. Words by themselves cannot fully communicate profound, philosophical truths. Even through art, particularly the three-dimensional form is capable of translating the subtleties of the philosophical principles by way of posture, flexion, ornamentations and facial expression; there are some aspects, which can only be communicated through the employment of specific symbols, which have associated meanings. A large numbers of wooden sculptures are noticed in the temples of the region. Each sculpture is carved in a folk style of the area. The three-dimensional freestanding sculptures are found in a very small number while those carved in relief on the wooden panels are innumerable. Both the types of sculptures are marked by unique expression. People have implicit faith in these sculptures. Their forms are not symbolic but representational. Each sculpture represents a well-known Hindu deity and is carved in strict adherence to iconographical tenets for immediate recognition. The master craftsman during the rhythm of creation projects his deep faith and religious belief in that very sculpture. It is due to the deep faith that it makes a lasting impact on the people. Three-dimensional sculptures usually represent the minor gods called (*beer)* and are placed in the small temples of the complex of the principal deity (Pl.40). These sculptures are carved out of a single block of wood and every effort is made by the carver to keep the grain of the wood intact. In wooden panel, the figures of the deity and events of life during various incarnations are carved with great artistic skill. Such relieves are carved on the small wooden panels and vary in size from few inches to many feet and are made to fix either on architectural members or placed in the niches of the temples.

In Banchoonch, the some wooden sculptures of gods and goddesses are also lying in the open in temple complex. The temple of the village deity is also decorated with woodcarvings. A sculpture showing Vishnu riding on his mount *Garuda* is carved with great deal and beauty (Pl.41). He is holding a disc and mace in his hand and resting his one leg on the shoulder of *Garuda.* The other sculptures such as *Mahishasurmardini* riding on lion, Śiva seating on bull and few other sculptures are also lying in the campus.

The other famous place for woodcarving is Jubbal. The palace of Raja Jubbal has intricate wood carving on the ceiling and a Devi temple at old Jubbal also is richly carved with floral and figural woodwork. In addition to these places there are several other temple, which have the carving on its architectural members. Gen. Godfrey Charles Mundy visited Jubbal on September 1828 and surprised to see the intricate wooden work at Devi temple at Deora(old Jubbal). He states, "Deora is, as its name would imply, a place of some sanctity. There is a very pretty modern temple, much ornamented with carved wood work". [10]

Besides these some mansions of royal families are also decorated with artistic woodcarvings. These spacious houses are carved externally on all four sides consisting of arches, pillars, balconies, windows, etc. while the interiors have carved windows frames, door jambs, door panels and ceiling, etc. The darbar hall of the Jubbal palace has intricate woodcarving on the ceiling. In the hall there are two beautifully carved flower vases which were executed by a woman carver named Moti.[11]

Some of the traditional concepts and basic techniques used in the woodcarvings are the representation of human, divine and animal forms. These are not direct copies of natural appearance (pratikriti), but the artistic expression of their intangible qualities and significance. In the same way, leaves, flowers, creepers and other floral designs are created from the essence of the forms rather than direct copies of their natural shape. Natural forms such as plants, flowers and leaves have special characteristics, such as graceful curves, groupings of buds, unfolding of flowers, their folding and creasing, the spiralling growth of plants, lustrous colour, delicacy and softness of various textures, etc. All these are observed, understood, well savoured and the response of the artist, expressed through his unique artistry and skill, and seen in his representation of plant forms in his works.

Natural forms thus, represented imaginatively and skilfully are known as *karukkani*. The rhythmic repetition of natural forms resembles the scattered edge of the saw used by the carpenter. The floral motifs are employed to ornament the various architectural features. Narrow strips in architectural features of buildings such as bands, columns and doorframes are adorned with the pattern of intertwined creeper and leaves. The stem of the creeper is shown curving, arching and curling. Along the side of the stem, leaves are represented with aesthetic grace. Among the flowers lotus, sunflower and rose are the some commonly used symbols in the ornamentation of the architectural members of the buildings. Lotus motif is employed very frequently in the temple architecture and also acts as a pedestal for the images of the deities. It is the symbol of divine origin and purity. The varying signification of the lotus arose out of its association with water, sun and the creation myth. As a water plant, it functions as an adequate symbol to suggest fertility or life giving powers of water and of creation. When the Supreme Being Narayana willed the creation a lotus shot up from his navel on which appeared Brahma, charged with the duties of creation. Lotus is further a symbol of solar because of its association with the sun

Many animals and birds have been represented in a graceful, imaginative manner in the architectural members. Among the animal figure lion, elephant, horse, bull and deer are commonly used symbols in woodcarving. The artist uses the lion motifs to characterize bravery. The form of the lion in sculpture is quite unlike the actual, realistic shape of a lion. The artist represents the attributes and various inherent physical characteristics of the animals skilfully, without restoring to copying the original. The lion possesses a powerful body built for swift movement. Elephants are a symbol of royal splendour and serve as a mount of state and purpose of magic. Horses are carved in the panels depicting the battle scenes while the bull and deer are represented as a vehicle of deities.

Another more interesting symbol used for the adornment of the temple is a '*purnaghata*, (water pot containing foliage) it is a symbol of abundance. In Jaina art the *purnaghata* is considered as one of the *Astamangala*, or eight auspicious symbols and also one of the fourteen lucky dreams of Tisala. In Buddhism it is considered as a auspicious symbol and represents Stupa.[12]

Masks[13] are the other types of carvings. Masks are used either on festive occasions or to portray character in dramatic performance and in re-enactment of mythological events. The mask carved out of wood, are typically primitive in appearance. In some of the mask the mouth is shown by a long slit. Ears are represented by raised wooden portion and eyes are represented as a shallow cavity. The backside is hollow and the mouth is stylistically represented with two rows of teeth. The masks are also carved with animal faces representing different species and vary in shape and size, which stands as an eloquent testimony of folk art of the area.

Besides the decoration of architectural members and making of images, wood has also been used in the past for utilitarian purposes like that of furniture, decorative artefacts, utensil etc. The utensils were hewn out of cylindrical wooden logs and were given a proper finishing and shape. Generally, these vessels were used for the storage of grains, churning the curd and kneading the floor, etc. The use of such artefacts for daily use is also mentioned in the Rig Veda[13]. Other Vedic text including the white Yajurveda and Atharvaveda also refer to wooden articles manufactured by the wood-carvers.

References:

1. X.81.4
2. Brown, Percy, *Indian Architecture, (Buddhist and Hindu)*, p.6 Rowland, Benjamin., *The Art and Architecture of India Buddhist-Hindu-Jain*, p.21.
3. Coomaraswamy, A.K., *The Arts and Crafts of India and Ceylon*, pp.163-164.
4. Watt, Sir George, *Indian Art,* p. 100.
5. Fraser, J.B., *The Himalaya Mountain,* p.166.
6. Malhans, B.S., Craftsmanship of Rohru- Chirgaon, Paper presented on a seminar on the History, Art and Archaeology of Himachal in Shimla. April,1998.
7. Chauhan, Hari, Hatkoti- a place of religious sanctity, *Marg magazine* vol.53, No.3, p.61.
8. Zimmer, Myths and symbols in Indian Art p.72, Percy Brown, Indian Architecture, p.116.
9. Malhans, B.S., Craftsmanship of Rohru- Chirgaon p. c (x) Paper presented on a seminar on the History, Art and Archaeology of Himachal in Shimla, April 1998.
10. Munday, G.C., *Pen and Pencil sketches, being the journal of a tour in India*, vol.1, p.310.

11. Singh Mian Goverdhan, *Art and Architecture of Himachal Pradesh*, p.24.
12. Coomaraswamy, A., *Yaksha*, p. 61.
13. X.101.7; I.84.18, I.110.6.

CHAPTER 7

JEWELLERY

Jewellery must have originated from man's innate desire for self-adornment. To fulfil this desire he adorned himself with ornaments fashioned from flowers, leaves, seeds and fruits, or pieces of bones, shells and ivory and sometimes with beads and precious stones, etc. With the discovery of metal, ornaments entered in the man's life in their most crude form. He started preparing the ornaments and jewellery from the metals like copper, iron and silver in addition to archaic material. It is attested with the discovery of large number of ornaments found in the excavation of various sites of the Indus civilization.[1]

We find some information about different types of jewellery worn by people in our Vedic literature.[2] The love of the Aryans for the jewellery is evident from the *Rigveda, According* to H. Clifford Smith, "The *Rigveda* mentions that the Maruts decorated themselves with various ornaments and shining necklaces and pendants on their breasts".[3] The main ornaments, which their deities wore, were the *van-mala, akshyamala, vaijantimala, rudraksh-mala, mund-mala, etc.* In the Epic we also find the mention of jewellery types worn during that period. In Ramayana we find details of jewellery while describing beauty and splendour of Sita. In Mahabharata, Arjuna in disguising their identity in the palace of Virata wore necklace, bracelets and earrings. According to the Manusmriti, the oldest Hindu treatise on social law, a woman's jewels are her *stri-dhan,* the only property legally and irrevocably owned by her. As their only insurance in a male-oriented, unsupportive social structure, and against the vicissitudes of time and old age, a woman tends to hold on to as much as possible and in earlier times safeguard it on her person. Brihatsamhita of Varahmihira contains the description of many varieties of pearl and their subtle powers.[4] The great poet Kalidass gives delightful description of the beauty of human figure enhanced by jewel and a more fascinating tradition is the use of gems as remedies for various ailments in the practice of the Ayurvedic system of medicine. Ratnavali of Harsha names the different types ornaments like for ear kundalas, Karna bharanas, karnotpalas, sesahara and tarathara for neck and mekhla for waist.[5]

A study of the representation of jewels in sculptures, carvings and paintings gives us an idea of their variety and importance from the Harappan period down to the present time. We can see a really fabulous display of jewels and ornaments, evidence of their essential role as symbols of heavenly glory, metal beauty and power. Silver, copper and gold have been used for ornaments since long time. However, the people still use some flower and leaves and bones for their adornment. The men adorn their caps with plumes of flower and ladies wear the necklace with a tigers claw[6] as pendent embedded in gold or silver and provided with hooks through which the chain is passed, and also tuck flowers in their hair buns. In Kinnaur district man and women also wears mala of chilgoza seeds during the occasion of marriage.

The ornaments worn by the woman provides an insight into their notions of beauty and adornment. Over the past few years change have taken place in socio-economic cultural life. A shift in traditional values has resulted in their moving away from their centuries old life style and old customs of loading oneself with heavy silver jewellery, is replaced with light and designed gold jewellery. Apart from old traditional ornaments, new designs and fashion always creep in for bringing about the change. This is responsible for declining taste of the people for old jewellery design. However the traditional forms are still remained the choice of the new generation. The gold, which has high face value, not only serve the purpose of adornment but also ensures the economic security for the lifetime. With the introduction of machine made jewellery in the market the people even prefer to prepare the traditional ornaments from the local goldsmith. Apart from the local gold market the jewellery of the area also established their place in the other market due to their beautiful designs and shapes. What ever may happen to the fashion or shapes of designs of jewellery, it is certain, that a woman's love of personal adornment will never completely fade in the years to come. It will remain forever. In this connection, K.de. B. Codrington's remarks produced in 'The handicraft and Industrial Art of India' seems to have justification:-"The fact that jewellery is a traditional form of wealth and that a man will hang his ear ring round his wife's neck and arms and anklets is not merely to be regarded as an unsocial antiquated form of hoarding. It is delightful and until the new word with its cooperative societies and school can give equivalent value in delight, it will certainly go on"

In that quest of love and beauty, there is not a part of women body which did not have a reason for beautified . The head, the forehead, the ears, the nose, the neck, the breasts, the arms the wrists, the figure, the ankle, the feet and the toes all were included. Nowhere else in India can we see such lavish use of jewels of precious metals in such lovely combination of colours and shapes, made to catch the light and reflect it in thousand sparkling ways, giving every movement a caress of beauty and gracefulness.

Technique of Manufacture: The local goldsmiths known as *Sunar* prepare the traditional jewellery. He works with a few instruments and tools. In spite of being equipped only with a set of old instruments, he produces fine jewellery. These instruments are very rough and seem crude but the art they produce are unique and magnificent. From fusing of metal to designing, enamelling, engraving, moulding and finishing of ornaments, the *Sunar* does everything personally. The jewellery of the area is made of the purest and finest material whenever they can be affordable and fashioned with all delicacy and elaborateness with the reach of the jeweler art. Pure gold, because of its softness, is rarely used. It is generally alloyed with copper, and silver with copper and zinc. The proportion of the alloy is not same at all places and in all types of ornaments. The tools used by the *Sunar* are similar types as used in the other part of the state. It consist of crucible (small clay dish), *angethi* (furnace), *nal* (blowpipe), *hathouri* (hammers), *sansi* (tongs), *zambur* (small pincer), *cheni* (chisels), *reti* (file), *nihai* (anvil), and *thappas* (dies) of various kinds shaped according to the nature of the ornaments. These *thappas* are used in bringing out the desired pattern by hammering.

Metal is melted in a crucible. Crucible is placed on the charcoal and a blast of air is given with blower. Flame of Charcoal of pine tree is considered best for heating the metal. In melting process care is taking that it should receive an even blast. When some vapours appears floating on the melted surface it is the indication to remove the crucible from the hearth. Before pouring the metal into a mould it is smeared inside with some oily substance so that the hot lump of solid metal may come out from the mould with a slight blow. Now the metal is ready which is ready to work on. If the quantity of the metal is less it is melted on asbestos paper or on a charcoal block. A blast of air is given through a curved blow pipe on a kerosene lamp flame.

Annealing: Gold and silver become harder by hammering or by drawing it often to make a wire out of it. In case the process is continued without re-heating the metal it is likely to break. To prevent metal from becoming brittle re-heating is done. This process of softening metal is called annealing and is locally known as *tao dena*. By doing this metal become ductile and easier to work on. While annealing a metal, *suna*r heat them to a dull red in between the soft flame of charcoal. While doing so a care is taken that the metal does not melt again. Metal is heated evenly by blowing a flame. Sunar judges well when to remove the metal from the forge after it has been evenly annealed. Heated metal is now left to cool it is never dipped into the water when it is red-hot. If this is done the metal loses its softness to some extent. In case of large pieces metal are held with pincers on one side and the hammering is taken up. When the pieces are small the artisan holds one end of the mildly hot metal in one hand while he shapes and works on it with the other. It is not necessary that the metal should be hammered soon after it looses redness. The annealed metal can be worked any time. There is no chance of its breaking or cracking. After 30-40 strokes, re-annealing required to avoid cracks or splits.

Designing: Annealed metals are shaped and designed step by step according to ornament. While preparing ornaments several types of silver or gold sheet and wire of different gauges and dimension are required. Metal sheets are cut into various shapes as may be required for an ornament. These shapes are again worked to form various depressions, concave and convex impression, ornamental and floral designs etc. Some time these sheets are carved with the heads of various animals according to shape and designs of the ornaments. For designing these ornaments a numbers of implements are required. Metal and wooden moulds for carving various depressions are required to give a round shapes to the sheet. For large depressions bossing hammers and mallets are used. For making small depressions the dapping tools called 'padernoo; is used. Engraving are done with pointed chisels, scrapers and scribers. For embossing of metals a number of iron and bronze dies are used. For repouse when designs are drawn engraving and embossing is taken up with scribers, having different cuts and with dappling tools of various sizes. This type of work is carried out mostly on ornaments like *chak, dhagle, sunangan* and pendants. Much of the *suna*r work is done by using the bell-metal dies (*thappas*) these have several patterns and shapes in them. It is the ingenuity of the craftsman in stamping out these designs on metal and then combining into in the form of an ornament.

Wires of different thickness and shapes are prepared and then plaited, knitted or twisted according to the designs. Thin wires are used for making chains, linear appliquéd shapes and oval hook links. Thick wire is used to make strips by hammering and cutting them according to design.

In certain ornaments like balu, bragar,long, murki and nath the setting of small pallets is done very artistically. In nose ornament *murki,* a fine trelliswork designed with ornamental setting of small grains is the excellent example of artistic excellence. These small pellets are prepared from a thin wire which is cut into small bits with special scissors called roala-banane-ka-katira. These small bits are placed in each groove of a specially prepared crucible, and become round pellets after melting.

Soldering: After shaping and designing different pieces of an ornament, these are deftly joined together. The process of joining pieces of metal is known as *tanke- ka- kam.* When soldering is done a specially prepared metal or *tanka* is placed between the joints. The whole piece is evenly heated this *tanka* has a lower melting point as compared to the metal that has to be joined. When the solder fuses at melting point it soon blends both the pieces and forms a firm joint. Solder (tanka) is prepared by goldsmith in different proportions. For silver, solder containing 3 *mashas* of zinc and 12 *mashas* of silver (trimas ka tanka) is considered as best. Solder prepared by adding 5 parts of zinc to 48 parts of silver is used for annealing work. The solder commonly used for gold soldering is prepared by adding 8 parts of gold and one part of either silver or copper or both. The solder commonly used for gold soldering is prepared by adding eight parts of gold and one part of either silver or cooper or both.

Preparation of solders: Solder is prepared by melting a gold and silver in a crucible. A small amount of borax is added. When the metal attains the molten state, other metals are added in certain ratio. The metal are then mixed in a crucible with an iron rod. The molten alloy is poured back into reja. The lump of alloy thus formed is flattened to form a thin sheet. Then the sheet is cut with snip, into very small oblong and square pieces. These tiny fragments are collected in a small container which contains borax powder. A few drops of water are poured to form a thin paste of it. This is called flux. Flux is then mixed with the bits of solder. The ornament which is to be soldered is also coated with flux. Then the scrap solder is placed on or between the joint with tweezers. The article is left to dry. Care is taken that it is warmed under a low heat. If heated abruptly bits of solder may fall. For this blow- pipes are used. This helps in throwing the heat at the right place. Sunar is careful that the heat is not directed at the solder; otherwise, tiny bits of solder may would melt and fall. Even if one part of joint receives heat enough for soldering and the other does not, the solder adheres only to the hottest part and the joint is not success. Great deftness is shown in carrying out the soldering job as there is a very minute difference in the melting temperature of the metal and solder.

Stamp designing: Much of the sunar's job is done by using steel and bell-metal dies. These have several patterns and shapes in them (Pl.42a,b). Some of these are used for preparing a particular ornament. Two of the bell metal dies called *titkara* and *bahuguna* are frequent use. Titkara is an oblong piece of bell metal, which has width-wise deep cuts of different design. Similarly, *bahuguna* is a circular piece of metal with geometrical design impression. Now it is the ingenuity of the craftsmen in stamping out these designs on a precious metal and then combining them into the form of an ornament. The sheet of the metal is first placed on the die and blows are given with plain hammer till the impression is received on the back of the metal. If the sheet is thin enough, a thick piece of lead is placed over the sheet and hammering is done. Some time the sheet of gold is as thin as a sheet of paper. To receive the impression on so thin sheet, cotton is used in place of lead. In this way, the thin sheet of silver or gold receives the designs. Before stamping out design on the metal sheet annealing is done so that there will be no breakthrough of the metal while hammering.

Repousse work: Repousse work is the process of decorating a metal sheet of gold or silver by carving designs on the reverse side of it and then turning the metal over and sharpening these designs on the face of it. The method, by which the relief is raised, is by hammering the sheet with scribers, and impression pens. In most cases the designs are drawn on a metal sheet with pencil. When the design is drawn, engraving and embossing works are taken up with scribers, having different cuts and with dapping tools of various sizes. This type of work is carried out mostly on ornaments like chak. bracelets, pendent, etc.

Enamel work: Enamelling is known as *Meena-kari.*[7] Enameled jewellery because of shining colour adds beauty to the ornaments. Enamel is a type of soft glass known as *meena* glass, is a composition of sand or flint with soda or potash. The fusion of these ingredients produces a transparent colourless glass. This becomes enamel. To produce enamelled ornaments this enamel is fused with certain verifiable mineral colors by heat on metal. These colors are found in the form of lumps, usually in green, blue and red.

First the ornament is thoroughly cleaned in tezab-ka-pani. The surface, where enamelling is required , is made rough by scrubbing and scratching. After that a coat of flux is given. Then the thick layer of wet powder is placed. The layer is kept even and slightly above the level of outlines or edges within which enamelling is needed. After the powder is spread, the piece of ornament is left to dry. When the piece is dried, the piece is carefully placed between the grooves prepared out of live coals. In case, the piece is delicate or small, it is placed on a clay-plastered tin plate. Then the fusing process is taken up. The coals are heated up and the piece is made red hot. The heating process is done swiftly to bring better result. Even heating of the entire piece is required during the process. When it becomes red hot , it is time for enamel to the fuse. The time taken in fusing varies according to the degrees of the enamel's hardness as well as of the thickness of the metal. After the enamelling a piece, filing, scrubbing, washing, brushing and polishing is done.

Pickling: Pickle is a technical term give to a solution of sulphuric acid and water. *Sunar* call it *tezab-ka-pani* or *tezab* and keep it in a glazed jar. This is prepared by adding one part of acid to ten to fifteen parts of water. As many times a piece of ornament receives heat it gets oxidised. If the oxidised metal is kept in the solution for about ten to fifteen minutes, the layer of oxide dissolves and the metal regain its lustre. When the piece is taken out of the solution, it is dipped in clear water. In the past when sulphuric acid was not available the artisans prepares a special home made pickle. It is prepared from wild apricot. These are boiled in a earthen pot. The water is strained. The solution is effective in removing the oxide scale and in making the solder joint hard.

Filling and polishing: When the ornament is in the final stage it requires finishing and polishing. Before this is taken in hand, the ornament is properly files and scrapped. This process removes edges, scratches, ball-up spot of solder and perfect surface and curves according to shape. The gold smith have a number of different needles files, some flat, round, half round, triangular, spear shaped and others with varying edges. Emery papers of different grades are also used. The artisans do this work with care, otherwise over filing may spoil the whole piece. The filing process makes the ornament ready for polishing and giving final touches. An especially prepared solution, red sand and soap nut are used for washing and polishing ornaments. Polishing is done with the help of sodium sulphate, alum salt, sulphuric acid, etc. mixed in required proportion. Ornaments are first boiled in this solution, washed with lean water and then brushed with glass brush. Wire brushes are also used for washing and polishing. In carved ornaments, only hand-polishing is done with the help of soap- nut water. To remove the wetness, ornament is put in lime-powder or saw dust. After all these process are over, the ornament become ready

Sunar use only few chemicals for preparing and cleaning the ornaments. *Suhaga*(borax) is universally used as a flux in melting metal, *amchur*, *nausadar*(Sal ammoniac) and *imeli* are used for cleaning and brightening and *manik-ret* (red dust) is also used for brightening the ornaments.

Types of Jewellery: In old times, traditional ornaments were made of silver but with the change of times and a social-economic condition, the silver was replaced with gold. The heavy jewellery of the silver is replaced with the light and designed gold jewellery. However, the traditional silver jewellery is still in use in the remote areas of the region. Woman with ornaments in ear, nose and arms were considered to be the representative of marital felicity, *sūhagun.* To be devoid of ornaments signifies widowhood or formal renunciation of worldly life. During the several fairs and festivals and marriages women put on their richest ornaments, at times their weight exceeding 8 Kg also. Some ornaments are put on the girl at the time of her marriage on a *subh-muhrat* by reciting hymn after which she said to attain the status of *suhagan*. It is obligatory for every married woman whose husband is alive to wear ornaments in the nose, ear and bangles in her hand and removed them only when she becomes widow. Amulet (jantar) of gold or silver containing piece of paper with certain mystical words written on it are worn in the neck by people to ward off effects of evil or black magic. Some corals and stones embedded in the rings and necklace are also worn to minimise the evil effect of *grahas and Nakshtras*. Gold is held precious and a sacred metal and is not worn in the feet. Woman of the area wear jewellery from head to her toe and during many occasions she remains laden with jewellery that produces the alluring effect on her personality and tinkling sound of the ornaments adds to grace in her movements(Pl.43). The ornaments worn by the women on their body is as under:

Head ornaments: Elaborate coiffeur has been the hallmark of women through every era. The preference for long black tresses still survives in the area. The head ornaments prevent the plait from unravelling. The ornaments worn on the hair plait, symbolizing the marital status of the women.

1. Chak: It is an ornament used on the hair plait on the back of the head. All married women wear it on their head symbolizing their *suhagan* status. Chak is prepared in both gold and silver. It is generally of convex shape and is about1/2 inch to 1 inch high with a diameter of about 2 inch 3 inch. Hooks are soldered on the inner side, which help it to be tied to the hair plait. It is necessary to every woman to wear this ornament on her head but the tradition is fading day by day and now it remains as a custom only and is worn on the day of wedding ceremony only.

2. Jutti: It is a silver hair pendent hung by the back of the head on a plait of hair. Jutti has several shapes and sizes. In some cases it is long and attached with the long cloth pockets where the plait of hair is put inside and silver chains are stitched in three or four rows joined with hook at short intervals giving it a decorative effect (Pl.44). At the end these chains were provided with cluster of drops, which produce jingling sound on the movement. In other form of jutti about six inches long hollow pipe thicker in the middle and conical towards the ends and is carved with some floral designs. In its middle and on the two ends oval hooks are soldered from which cluster of drops are hung. Jutti is generally prepared in silver and weighing about

350gm to 500 grams. This ornament is generally worn during the festive occasion and on other days it is replaced with cotton jutti.

3. Hair pin: The women use it just above the ears to tie her hairs. Hairpins are usually made of silver or gold with many geometrical and floral designs. It helps the women to unravel her tresses. It is about 3 "long and 1.5" wide. On the back a pin and a hook is provided by which it is tied to the hair.

Ornament for forehead: The ornament for the forehead is a *singar-patti (shingar-patti)*, a plate-like ornament of a broad strip of two knitted chains fringed with globular metals beads. Other design of the ornament is knitted together to form a rectangular plaques in a row. It is either made of silver or gold. When *singar-patti* of silver has a central circular pendent with *ghunrus* or *pipal* leaves suspended from it, then it is called *chidi*. The silver disc of *chidi* is decorated with *meena* work (enamelling).

Mantika or *Mangtika* or *tika* consists of a large circular disc, which comes right over the forehead. It is engraved with floral motifs and the *pipal* leaves are suspended from the lower half of it. The diameter of the plaque varies from five to six centimetres. It displays number of designs and is made of gold (fig.46). A different type of popular *tika* comes in the shape of crescent moon. It is called *argh-chandru* or *chandru (ardha-chandra)*, meaning half moon. On this crescent shape, either one-cut piece of stone is fixed or the surface is decorated with the motifs of flowers, rosettes or with blue, white and red imitation stones. It is generally worn on the side of the forehead and is made of gold.

Ear ornaments: Ear ornaments are an important constituent of female attire. The range and variety of ear ornaments of the region are different than that of anywhere else in the state. An extraordinary range and variety of forms and designs could be seen worn by the women. To the married woman the ear ornament is auspicious, whereas, bare earlobes signal widowhood.

In addition a woman wealth conspicuously visible and the ear ornament became the statement of her status and power, elongated ear lobes since very old times were considered a sign of beauty and health.[8] By appending ornaments to almost every part of ear, the woman also, ensures a continuous state of mental and physical well-being. Some of the popular ear ornaments are as under:

1. Bragar: It is a large gold ear-ring with two round pearls and a conical turquoise suspended in the center(fig46a). The conical turquoise is called *neelak.* Generally these are of red and green color. Some portion of the pearls and turquoise is encrusted with the fine trelliswork prepared from the grains of gold. From the central turquoise occasionally three or five small drops are hung. Just close to pearls about half an inch portion of the ring on both sides is covered with a coiled thin wire. Half the portion of the ear-ring is a thick wire without any decoration. At one end a hook is fitted and an oval link provided at the other end of the ornament. Bragar are prepared of gold and silver and in size one-inch diameter to two inch and weigh between 15 grams to 40 grams a pair.

2. Darotu: A peculiar shaped earring prepared in gold and is worn on the lobe of the ear. It is made of single long wire. The half part of this wire is bent round to form a ring with a small closed hook at one end (46b). The remaining part is turned outward to form a semi-circle. Here another inward bend is given. Now the wire is turned round and round to form three to five circles each shorter than the previous one. A pair weighs about 15-25 grams.

3. Kāntae: These are prepared in several geometrical designs and are about 1.5 to 3 inch long. The long *kānṭā* is provided with a thin long chain with a tiny oval link at one end. The ornament is prepared in gold and silver and each weighs between 1.5 to 2.5 grams.

4. Karan-phul: It is commonly used ornament and is prepared in gold and silver. It is either enameled or chased cone plaque, some time fitted with turquoise in the center. Its outer edge resembles like a star or is sometime appliquéd with a wire ring having impressions of jound knobs

5. Bālian: It is an ear- ring with beautiful decoration work. A crescent shaped piece of embossed metal is fitted to the wire by a hinge at one end and hook on the other. The lower edge is extended with a wirework carrying flat or round piece of metal at a certain regular gap. Its pair normally weighs about 15 to 30 grams. It is normally worn on the lobe of the ear. Balian are prepared both in silver and gold and even poor women wears brass metal also.

6. Dāndi: It is an earring. The only decoration in it is the coiled thin wire, which encircles about half the portion of the ring. This is prepared in gold and silver and weigh from 5 to 10 grams. The *dāndis* are worn on the upper lobe of the ears.

7. Murki: Small earrings, particularly worn by men in the lobes. It is prepared both in gold and silver and weigh in few grams.

8. Gokhru: It is an ear ring always of gold. It has three beads on its three corners and joined with small hollow rods(Pl.46c). The central bead is larger than other two beads. At the upper portion hinge and hook is provided, wherein a curved wire is fixed by which it is hung to the earlobe. It has different Sizes and shapes and weight of the ornaments varies from 10grams to 25 grams.

Nose ornaments: There is no early sculptures and painting showing the women either wearing anything in the nose or with pierced nose. Perhaps the custom gained universal popularity in the later period. Now it is impossible to find a girl with an un-pierced nose. Dr. P.K. Gode is of the view that use of nose ornament begins in 10th century A.D. and it is a foreign importation into Indian Culture.[10] While A.S. Altekar establishes that the nose ornament comes in fashion with the Muslim.[11] But K. Krishnamurthy in his book "Mirror of Indian Culture" argues that terracotta figurine discovered at Chagtur reveals a nose ornament and figurine dated to Satvahana period of 1st–2nd century A.D. A female figure from Nagarjunakonda which dates back to 3rd century A.D. is shown wearing a nose ornament. In some *mithuna* couple of Nagarjunakonda, male lover is shown adjusting the nose ornaments of his beloved while she is shown looking at the mirror.[12] Amongst many jewels with which the woman adorns herself, the nose ornament is perhaps the most seductive. This evidently indicates that the nose ornament was known to the Indian in early time as early as in 1st –2nd century A.D. Ornaments for the nose take on a variety of shapes ranging from tiny jewelled stud to the large gold hoops that encircled the cheek with graceful pendent pearls dangling provocatively just above the upper lip. It is mandatory for married woman to wear the nose ornament every time.

1. Tili: It is common ornament worn by the woman on her nose. It is generally of gold and weighs hardly few grams. It is produced in varying designs. Some have plain surfaces and a decorated edge. Some are appliquéd with three or more imitation stones. Some are decorated with grain works. Others are fitted with simple turquoise or red stones in the centre having grain work all round. It is round and slightly conical with a long hollow pin provided at the back. The hollow pin is inserted inside the nose and fitted with sliver pin known as *kulfi*.

2. Phulli: It is worn in the nose like tili. It is a star shaped or circular stud with small jewels or *nug* fitted in the centre and some time all around, as well. The hollow pin is inserted inside the nose and fitted with sliver pin known as *kulfi*.

3. Karolu: It is suspended from the nose and looks like a decorated disc. At the upper portion hinge and hook is provided, wherein a curved wire is fixed by which it is hung to the septum. Sizes, shapes and weights of this ornament are varying. It is also known as bulāk in other part of state.

4. Bālu: It is a large ring worn on the nose. This is ornamented with a belt of jewel or pearls. Some of the jewels are encased into grain-worked semicircular balls, through which the ring wire passes(Pl.47). Another design is prepared by fitting flat round plaque to the half portion of wire ring with one or two pearls in the centre. The ornament is quite heavy and weighs about 20to 60 grams. Due to its heavy weight and big size its shorter version called *nath* [13] replaces this ornament.

5. Kokā: It is a substitute of a tili weighing less than a gram. This is a gold knob with a hollow pin to which another pin is fitted from inside the nose. Generally a small red stone known as *thewa* is fixed on the knob.

Ornaments for neck: Ladies are very fond of neck ornaments. The variety and range of neck ornament is very vast. The traditional neck ornaments were of silver and the weight of these ornaments was very heavy. Now these ornaments are prepared in gold in lightweights and the traditional shapes stand replaced by the modern designs. The traditional neck ornaments are as under:

1. Hansali- It is a large silver collar made of solid metal. It is worn around the neck. It is prepared from half an inch square or a round bar and its circumference may be about 15" to 20". Its central half is comparatively thick. Its two ends are shaped to the form of a round knob, which are sometimes given an outward turn. It is decorated with geometrical designs in the central portion and weighs about 150 to 350 grams. In the other part of the country it is also known as Hansauli.[14] In the early sculpture we find a yaksha sculpture from Mathura dating to 1st century B.C. is shown wearing this old ornament. In the valley we also noticed some sculpture wearing this type of jewellery.[15]

2. Satlari hār - It is a silver necklace usually worn by the women during the old time but in some part of the area this ornament is still popular among the women. This traditional ornament is now replaced with the gold necklace of the modern designs. The *satlari hār* contains seven chains or some time more or less is added. Chains are prepared from several star shaped units with a flat round surface in the center. These units are linked each other with an oval link. The ends of these chains are linked to a triangular plaque with a fine trelliswork. One side of both the plaque is provided with as many oval hooks as may be required according to the number of chains. At the opposite corner another oval link is soldered. These two oval links are connected to long chains, which help to suspend the necklace from the neck. This type of necklace is prepared in a number of designs also. The fall of the seven chains comes one above the other on the breast lend charm.

3. Chandra-hār- This necklace is worn throughout the area. The ornament consists of several silver chains linked together by a pendant and plaques, which are enamelled or consist of simple silver bands (Pl.48). The chains are strands of tiny silver rosettes. The plaques are generally enamelled in blue and green. Sometimes one to five plaques with fine enamel work are in set in between the chains. Its weight varies from 400 grams to 2.5 kilograms. Now this type of necklace is replaced with light and designed goid necklace.

4. Trimani- The ornament contains three hollow gold beads of big size in the center and is appliquéd with grain work. A copper sheet is fixed inside for strengthening of beads. These beads are threaded in the center and the sides are added with seven or more string of small beads and provided with joint screw at the end.

5. Jantar- It is a silver necklace prepared in rectangular or square shape and is also known as *Tabeet*. It is worn to encase a 'Yantra' drawn on paper to keep off ill effects of witch-craft. It is outer surface is encrusted with fine trelliswork of grains. On the lower edge of the plaque is provided with hooks from which are suspended bunches of globular beads. At the opposite edge two oval hooks are soldered through which colored tread or silver chain passes and tied at the back of the neck. In Pandva sculpture of Valley dating to 14th –15th century they are shown decked with this ornament.

6. Hamel- It is a necklace of coins.[16] Old silver coins of are used to make the ornament. In the ancient Hindu texts, it is mentioned that both men and women used that ornament.[17] The coins are provided with an oval link at the edge just over the effigy head. The link is soldered here. Through the oval link thread is passed which gives it a form of a necklace (Pl.49). The effigy's head form the upper side of the ornament. Normally coins of uniform denomination are used. Sometime in the middle a big betel leaf shaped plaque of silver with stamp decoration is suspended. In some part of valley is also called *jothru*. The ornament weighs 100 to 150 grams.

7. Kantha- It is necklace of silver beads worn close round the neck. Beads are threaded in a cotton string so as to tie it round the neck. Ornament weighs about 50 to 100grams.

8. Champakali- It a necklace of several unit prepared by stamping a silver sheet on die cast. Both the end of the unit is pointed . At one end an oval link is soldered through which a long thread is passed so as to give it a form of a necklace.

Ornaments for the wrist: To women, ornaments for the wrist have always been significant emblem of marriage. More than any single jewellery the bangles has been crafted from the widest variety of materials. Ancient fragments testify that bangles were made from terracotta, shells, copper, bronze, gold, silver and almost any material that lent itself to craftsmanship. A woman never allows her arms to be completely bare. The popular wrist ornaments of the area are as under:

1. Gajroo- It is popular silver ornament of the old period worn by women. It is a hollow bracelet with teeth decoration on its upper surface (Pl.50). Pointed teeth are set in two or four lines. Inner lines are slightly longer than the outer sides. It has a flexible joint and has a close fit over the wrist. A pair of *gajroo* weighs about 150 to 200 grams.

2. Sunangan- It is a round bracelet prepared from gold. It is thin and plain in the middle and widened toward the end. The ends are engraved with the shape either of lion or *makra* heads (Pl.51a). The weight of one pair varies from 50 to 100 grams.

3. Dhaglae- It is a silver bracelet like *sunangan* (Pl.51b). The newborn baby is also arrayed with small and lightweight bangle. It is also provided with cluster of jhumkās, which produce jingling sound with the movement of arm.

4. Toke- It prepared from gold or silver plate, four centimeters wide and one-eighth centimeter thick, moulded into a circular shape, leaving a gap between the two ends, which can be adjusted. The upper surface of it is covered with the design of hallowed cucumber seeds in two or four rows.

Ornaments for finger: Like the other ornaments of body parts the finger ornaments are also equally important ornament. Finger ornament is very popular from very ancient time. In the Indus sites the rings made up of bronze, copper, shells and terracotta are found in excavation. There are several references of wearing finger ornaments in the literary sources of the Vedic period.[18] The tradition of wearing finger ornament is equally popular in the epic age.[19] A female figure from Barhut of Shunga period portraying a lady adorned with rings in all fingers. The women are very fond of the finger ornaments; one can find many women in the area wearing the rings in all the fingers.

1. Ring- The simple ring is not ignored in the vast array of larger ornament form. It is a common ornament worn by both men and women at almost all times. The ring worn by the men are comparatively heavier and bigger then that of women. It is usually made of gold, silver and copper. It is either of simple designs or provide with ornamental designs. Sometime ring are fitted with precious stones and jewels to minimize the evil effect of *grahas* and *Nakshatras* .

2. Arsi- Arsi[20] is a thumb-ring prepared by setting in it a round mirror on a large round metal frame, having a decorative border. This ornament is prepared both, in silver and gold. Unfortunately it is now falling into disuse. When this ornament appears in smaller size and shape, it is called *arsu.*

Waist ornament- Women also wears waist belt known as *gachhi* on her waist. The ornament consists of a number of chains held together by bands. This type of ornament also finds mention in the Ramayana as '*Kanchidama*'[21] or 'mekhla'.[22] There are large number of Sculpture, Paintings and carvings showing female wearing waist ornaments. The waist ornament worn by female is known by different names like Kanchi, Mekhla, Saptaki, Rashna and Sarsana etc. in different literarily sources.[23] It serves the dual purposes by holding the lower garment and helping to keep the backbone straight. It also serves to embellishment to the feminine force. It is traditional ornament worn only during the festive occasion while other days long cotton cloth serves this purpose. Such type of costumes is frequently noted on all sculptures. The width of the *gachhi* is 4 to 6 inch and weigh from 2 to 2.5 kilograms.

Ornaments for the ankles and toes- All the *suhagan* women wear the ornaments in their ankles and toes. The tradition of wearing the ornament in the ankle is very ancient there is large number of sculpture portraying the female figures wearing the anklets. The yakshi sculptures of Barhut and Sanchi are adorned with anklets. There are number of sculptures and wood carvings in the valley dating to 8th –9th century showing the female deities with this popular ornament. These ornaments are symbols of married status of the female. Ankle ornaments are always made of silver or copper but not of gold. By wearing gold in ankle it is disrespect to this precious metal.

1. Panjeb: *Pajeb* is a Persian word, meaning an ornament for the feet. In the local dialect, it is termed as *panjeb*. It is prepared by knitting a wire into an ornamental way. A belt of small and large drops is linked on the lower edge of the knitted piece. A clasp is also provided at the two ends, which makes it to fit on the ankle. It produces jingling sound on the movement.

2. Polaree: These silver rings are worn on toes. These rings either be simple or provided with small silver flat piece at the top and enameled with red, blue or green.

References:

1. Marshal, Sir Johan, Mohan-jo-daro and the Indus civilisation, Vol. II,1931, p. 528-529 and Vol. III, 511-513, 519, 522, 527, 531.
2. Rigveda, The Karnaśobhana an ornament for ear VIII. 78.3, Kūrira an ornament worn by female specially bride, X. 85.8, Atharvaveda, VII 138.2, 138.3, XV.2.1,Yajurveda, Niska, an ornament for neck XXII.1, Śatpatha Brahmaṇa VI.7.1.7. The necklace of round discs worn by Lakshna Devi, Shakti Devi and Nandi images (7th century A.D.) of Bharmour, Chamba are known as 'Dinar mala' which is termed as *nishka* in the Veda.
3. Clifford, H. Smith., *The Art of Jewellery*, Delhi, 2002, p.1.

4. Chap.81,VV.31-35.
5. Ratnavali, Act III, pp.22, 61, 74, 81, 114, 135, 139, 176 and 206.
6. The earliest reference of tiger's tooth as neck ornament in iconography is to be found in stone images of Kertikeya (see Illustration pl. XVII (i) and pl. XVII (ii). The Development of Hindu Iconography, J.N. Banerjea.
7. "There is no mention of enamelling in early Indian texts before the 15th-century. The only available reference found in this subject is in the *Ain-i-Akbari*, written in 16th-century by Abu'l Fazl, during the reign of the Mughal Emperor Akbar." Sharma Rita Devi and Varadarajan M., *Handcrafted Indian Enamel Jewellery*, New Delhi, 2004, p.11.
8. In ancient Indian text elongated ear lobes were considered to be the one out of 36 lakshanas of mahapursta.
9. The *Karanpul* as ear stud is frequently mentioned in the ancient Hindu literature. The ear ornament, resembles a flower of marigold, is referred to be worn by the image of Shalabanjika belonging to Kushan period. The ear ornament of the same design but in smaller in size are shown adorning by a female image in the collection of Mathura Museum. These (ear stud) are identified with ear ornaments *karnaphul* and *karnapur*, mentioned in the literary work of this period. Pandey Indu Prabha's , *Dress and Ornaments in Ancient India*, Varanasi, p160.
10. Gode, P.K., The antiquity of the Hindu nose ornament called' Nath' Annals of Bhandarkar, July, 1938, p.313-34.
11. Altekar, A.S., Dress and Ornament of the Hindu Women, BHU Journal-1938.
12. Clifford, H. Smith, *The Art of Jewellery* (Ancient and Modern Period), p.14.

13. Altekar, A.S., draw its origin from the word '*Anath*' mentioned in *Deshinammala* (4/17) 'Anathanasarju'. Dress and Ornaments of Hindu women, Journal of BHU, 1938.
14. During the Kushan and Gupta period the *hamsuli* was popular and there it was worn close to the neck. Pandey Indu Prabha, op.cit., pp.165, 197.
15. Bhushan, Jamila Brij, Indian Jewellery, Ornaments and Decorative Designs, pl. X, Pl.2.
16. The images of Nandi, Lakshana Devi and Ganesh at Brahmaur and that of Shakti Devi at Chitrari, are shown wearing a this kind of ornament and known as *dinar-mala*.
17. Pandey Indu Prabha, *Dress and Ornaments in Ancient India*, a necklace made of gold or silver coins, which was termed as *niska,*, op. cit. p.129.
18. Rigveda, 1/35/9.
19. Virat Parva, 32/13, 62/11 Karnparva, 58/5.
20. *Arsi* is a Hindi word, which means a mirror.
21. Sundrakanda, 9th sarga.
22. Ayodhyakanda, 78 sarga.
23. Acharya, Bhawna., *Prachin Bharat mein Rupshringar*, p.129.

CHAPTER 8

CONCLUSION

The political and art history of a place does not remain isolate from its economic, social, religious, cultural and ideological base and same holds true of the Pabbar Valley. The discovery of pottery, coins, inscriptions, art, architecture and later historical records suggest that there was a continuous migration of people from the plains to the mountainous region. The migration took place because of chaotic conditions prevailing in the region. This process further accelerated with the pressure of Muslim invasion. There are many races and homogenous groups like Khashas, Thakurs, Kanets and Brahmins who migrated from the different parts of plains to this hilly region and established their own political and cultural set up which is also reflected in their art, social and religious life.

In medieval period many small Thakuris came into existence but soon lost their identity with the rise of strong Rajput states. The political history of the region took new turn with the devastation of Sirmouri tal in 1095A.D. The valley fall in the hand of local renowned Brahmin and later his sons divided the area into three independent states. But later the heir of Sirmour once again extended their power in the valley and took the entire area under their control. Soon after in the 14th century Garhwal also extended its power and captured the Rawin fort and made it the fief state. The cis-Pabbar area remained under Sirmour, the Jubbal and Sairi remaining a feudatory vassal. There was continuous fight between Bushair, Sirmour and Garhwal to bring the area of Pabbar under their supremacy but no one succeeded until the Gurkha forces overran the entire valley in 1810A.D. With the expulsion of Gurkhas by the English forces in 1815 A.D the area of valley was divided between the Jubbal, Sari, Rawin, Bushair, and Garhwal state except for the few villages of Rawin state. After the India gaining independence in 1947 the valley became an integral part of Himachal Pradesh

An ancient trade route starting from Kalsi to Hatkoti and then on Rampur Bushair and leading to Central Asia was responsible for assimilation of different traits and style in the art and architecture. Thus cultural and artistic activity of the area was influenced under the various impacts in particular period.

The survey clearly reveals that the art of *nagara* temple was introduced in the valley from Central India in the early 8th century AD. During the reign of Yashovarman of Kanauj and Chand dynasty of Garhwal they find their closest affinity. The *nagara* style of temple architecture seems to penetrate this region during Pratiharas who were ranked as the supreme power in north India during 9th-11th century AD. Pratihara rulers were mainly responsible for construction of large number of stone temples in the north India. They had deputed their governors in the different parts of the territory under their control and patronized the art activities. It was the period when Shankrachrya revived the Hinduism and founded the four *pitha* in the four corners of India. The *nagara* temple found in the valley shows close resemblance with the temples of Garhwal, Kumaon and Central India. The style and design as well as chronology of temples admit of four phases of temple building activity noticed in the region roughly covering the period from 7th century to 13th century AD. The temple plan which was rudimentary in its earlier phase as we see in the miniature temples became more evolved in plan and elevation and its architectural members richly embellished in the subsequent period. The temples which can be listed in the first phase are those of miniature shrines found at Hatkoti, Parhat and Bachoonch which also served as models for large temples. The plans of these temples are simple and bereft of architectural designs. There is no ornamentation of any kind on their doorways, pillars, and other architectural members. Temples in this phase follow the '*dvianga*' ground plan, the doorway though divided into many *shakhas* is plain with occasional appearance of Ganesha on the *lalatbimba.* The *antrapatra* marking the division between the perpendicular wall of the *jangha* and curvilinear *shikhra* is a simple recessed band(pattika) and imposition of the *shikhra* above shows marked absence of corner *amalkas* and is composed of compressed tiers of *bhumis*. The mouldings of the *vedibandha* are worked out on a single mana-sutra.

In second phase, the temples gain height and the *bhadra* (wall niches at the cardinal points) are decorated with well-chiselled and detached sculptures of the gods related to the main deity in the sanctum (avrṇa-rupa-shobita). In some temples, *bhadra* are provided with a two-pillar portico (rathika). Architectural designs starts appearing, and the pillars, gateways, and *shikhras* are decorated with *ratna* and *ardha-ratana*(half diamond), *Purna-ghata*(vase of plenty), meandering creepers(patra-lata) and other floral and geometrical designs.

In third phase, temples are built on square platform (jagati), *panch-ratha*(with five offsets) in plan and elevation, and amply provided with *bhadras, pratibhadra* (offset-flanking bhadras), and k*arnas* (angles). Each *karna* is provided with a *bhumi amlaka* (cogged wheel marking the story of a shikhra). The process of stone temples building continued under the patronage of imperial powers till 12th century A.D. but with the withdrawal of patronage, the traditional wooden architecture once again attained popularity.

In a forested region like Himachal Pradesh wooden art was considered as indigenous art flourishing in harmony with its varied climatic conditions and becoming refined and elaborate with the lapse of time. Wood because of its easy availability was a material of choice not only for the edifices of ornamental character like temples but also for domestic and secular architecture. But unfortunately it being of perishable by natures temple did not survive for long, hence their outer shell does not predate 16th century. The wooden pent-roofed temple which Herman Goetz (*Studies in the History of Kashmir and Western Himalayas*, p.130) considers a prototype of Gupta period temple was transformed later into multi tiered pyramidal or pagoda style which entered from the Satluj valley with the strengthening of power of Bhushair ruler in the valley.

The sculptures found in the valley reflect the spiritual aspirations of the people of the particular period. During *bhakti* movement image worship asserted its overpowering influence. The age witnessed prolific growth of Puranic and Agama literature. Accordingly, a wide range of sculptural association with different sect of this period has been found from the region. However, most of the sculptures belong to *Brahmanical* divinities, particularly, *Vaishnava Shaiva* and *Shakta* sect. Transmission of various artistic traditions in the valley from different quarters helped in evolving a comprehensive art-style of this period. The sculptures of the valley mostly executed in buff sand stone, wood or cast in metal, show delicate modelling and refinement of carving. The sculpture of early 8th century reveal that they possess the plastic austerity and stylistic sophistication of the post Gupta period. The figures have hypnotic expression in their eyes with gently arched eyebrows, soft smile, and dignified expression on the marvellously rounded face and mildly upturned corners of lips. The elegant, chaste, discrete, long-limbed and expressive figures recall late Gupta mannerism as found in the sculptures of Parhat temples.

In the middle of 10th century A.D. the introduction of divinities with attendant figure instead of a single figure and elaborate *torna prabhavali* as we find in the sculptures of Durga temple complex and Bachoonch are some of the salient feature of the Pratihara art discernible in the sculptures. One of the marked peculiarities of most of the sculptures embellished in temple is the fine quality of the carving and the beautiful proportions and movement of the image. A love for increasing ornamentation can be felt, but it does not mar the sublimaty of the figures. The sculpture of this period reached a height of grace which was never touched by the later work. The metal sculpture of Mahishasurmardini enshrined in Durga temple Hatkoti has been considered by common consent as one of the finest specimen of Pratihara art in Himachal. The sculptures 0f 11th -12th centaury AD generally develop a tendency of heaviness in execution characterised by a little harness in lines anticipating the trend of mannerism towards folk style which are noticed in large number in different part of valley i. e Hatkoti, Masli, Rohru and Bachoonch etc.

The region also abounds in various types of memorial stones serve as an important historical record. These stones evoke their association with certain stages of the social and economic evolution of the society. They also provide a constant endeavour to search out parallels with the societies in the same or very similar stages of evolution. The memorial stones eventually throw some light on the deceased for whom the stones were erected.

Wood being a material widely used for ornamentation of building made it possible for the carver to design various artistic forms and designs. Because of its smooth texture and fine grain, its accessibility to bend and assume any shape it was possible for the carver to design various artistic forms and designs, which were elaborated and refined under the impact of various styles with the course of time. The wooden craft was also influenced by the artistic trends of the neighbouring regions that resulted in the assimilation of few new ideas and patterns. However, the working style remained unchanged even with the introduction of new ideas and techniques adopted from its surrounding and the new patterns and symbols were included to fulfil the aspirations and taste of local people. The panels which were initially delineated with the traditional patterns now were embellished with floral and geometrical design with the advent of Mughal architectural and decorative elements. The introduction of cusped arches decorated with spandrils and embossed with lotus rosettes, the mehrabs, bay windows, lotus pillars emerging from the lotus cups and terminating again into inverted lotuses, Mughal *jalis* especially used in elbow-rest fencing around the pradakshina path.

The art of jewellery over the past few years has undergone tremendous transformation with the change of socio-economic condition and life style of the people. A shift in traditional values has resulted in their moving away from their century's old customs and traditions and loading oneself with heavy silver jewellery. It is now replaced by light, cheap and attractively designed glittering jewellery. However the traditional designs are still remain their choice. Gold, which has high face value, not only serves the purpose of adornment but also ensures the economic security for the lifetime. With the introduction of machine made jewellery in the market, people nevertheless prefer the traditional ornaments and get them prepared from the local goldsmith. There is a great demand of traditional jewellery in the market especially among the visitors from out side who find them very attractive and wish to cherish them as souvenir of having visited the place. What ever may happen to the fashion or shapes of designs of jewellery, it is certain, that a woman's love of personal adornment will never completely fade in the years to come.

GLOSSARY

Abhaya mudrā	gesture made with raised right hand signifying protection
Adhiṣṭhāna	basement; the socle on which the temple stand
Akṣamālā	rosary of beads
Āliḍha mudrā	an archer's posture, the right knee being kept in the front and left stretched in attitude of shooting
Āmalaka	flattened ribbed or cogged stone
Antarāla	constricted vestibule
Antrapatra	the recess between the wall below and the curvilinear spire above and the recess between the mouldings
Ardha paryaṅka	a sitting posture, to sit with one leg crossed on the seat , the other one dangles along it
Ardharatna	half diamond decorative motif

Atibhanga	Accutuanted body posture
Āyudhapurusha	the personification of emblems of Vishnu in an anthromorphic form
Bhadra	cardinal projection
Bhadra mukha	the single or three faces of Shiva appearing on the caitya dormer
Bhiṭṭa	base slab
Bhūmi	compressed storey, horizontal course of storeys
Chaitya	a Buddhist shrine, a type of dormer or pediment decoration
Chakra	discuss, one of the emblems of Vishnu
Candraśālā	a decorated arched niche
Chatursara	four cornered
Chatra	parasol
Cymarecta	inverted lotus by pattern
Ḍamarū	small drum in the form of an hour-glass
Daśāvatāra	ten incarnation of Vishnu
Dhammilla	a type of hair-do
Dhotī	drapery, the lower garment
Dvārapāla	door- keeper
Dviaṅga	a temple having two proliferations
Ekāvalī	a hara of single variety

Gajapithā	a frieze of elephant
Gaṇa	grotesque dwarf goblin
Garbhagṛha	sanctum sanctorum
Ghaṭa pallava	vase and foliage motif
Grīvā	neck of the super structure
Hāra	necklace
Jāḍya kumbha	a variety of kumbha , a type of moulding
Jaṭā	matted hair
Jagatī	basement
Jaṅghā	the wall part of a temple
Kalaśa	vase; crowning member of a spire
Kamaṇḍalu	an oblong water- vessel with a handle and a spout
Kapilī	a short of projection in front of a cella
Kapota	a section of circular moulding made in the form of a pigeon's
Kapotapālī	a crowning moulding; cornice
Karṇa	corner
Karṇāmalaka	miniature āmalaka at the end of each bhūmi on a superstructure
Karṇika	a moulding of the vedībandha
Khura	hoof, a moulding

Kirīta mukuṭa	a ornamental conical crown with a central pointed knob
Kīrtimukha	an ornamental design with a lion mask figures and foliage
Kumbha	a moulding of vedībandha
Lalāṭbimba	image on the centre of lintel of sanctum's door
Makara	crocodile
Mālā	garland
Maṇḍapa	hall
Mātuluṅga	a kind of fruit
Mūla mañjarī	the main tower found within the encircling uruśṛṅgas
Mūla prāsāda	sanctum
Mūrti	image
Nāsikā	projection at the base of the superstructure on the main direction of orientation of a temple
Nīlotpala	the blue lotus
Pañaratha	temple structure with five vertical offsets
Paṭṭikā	a moulding of the platform; a band
Pedyā	lower part of the door-jambs
Pīṭha	base
Prāggrīva	narrow entrance porch

Pūrnaghaṭa	full vase motif
Rathikā	framed panel
Ratna pātra	gem-vessel
Sāndhāra prāsāda	a shrine which has a closed ambulatory between the inner sanctum wall and the surrounding exterior wall
Śikhara	spire or superstructure of a temple
Śrivasta	an auspicious symbol on the chest of Viṣṇu
Stambha	pillar
Stūpi	topmost part of a temple including kalaśa and the finial proper
Śukanāsikā	niche with caitya, dormer in front of the Śikhara
Toraṇa	an ornamental gateway at the very entrance into the temple unit
Tri-ratha	temple structure with three vertical offset
Udgama	pediment
Udīcya veśa	northern dress
Urdhaliṅga	ithyphallus
Urusṛṅgas	half Śikharas found on the sides of the main tower
Utkuṭikāsana	a sitting posture keeping with heel close to bottom and back slightly curved
Uttaraṅga	architectural part above the main door-frame of the sanctum

Uttarīya	upper garment
varaṇḍikā	cornice occurring over the wall of the temple
Vedībandha	moulding of the vase
Vījapūraka	a kind of fruit , crowning member over the spire
Vyāla	hybrid lion

BIBILIOGRAPHY

Agni Purāṇam, tr. M.N.Dutt Sastri, 2vols., Varanasi,1967

Kautilya-The Arthashastra, tr. L.N. Rangarajan, Penguin Book India, New Delhi, 1992

Baudhāyana Gṛhyasūtra., Ed. R.Shamasastri, Mysore, 1920

Bṛhatsamhitā, Ed. H.Kern, Calcutta, 1865

Kalhan's Rajatarangini, tr. Stein Aural, Delhi, 1961

The Śrîmad Devî Bhâgawata, tr. Swami Vijnanananda, 2nd ed., New Delhi, 1977

Vishnudharmottara, part III, tr. Stella Kramrish, 2nd ed., Calcutta,1928

Books

Acharya, Bhawna : *Prachin Bharat main Rupshringar*, Jaipur, 1995

Agarwal, P.K. : *Studies in Indian Iconography*, Jaipur, 1994

Agarwal, V.S. : *Indian Art,* Varanasi, 1965

: *The Heritage of Indian Art*, Varanasi, 1964

: *Evolution of the Hindu Temple, Indian Civilisation, Series*-V, Varanasi, 1965

Alkazi, Rosha : *Ancient Indian Costumes*: N.B.T.I. New Delhi rpt. 1998

Allan, J. : *Catalogue of the coins of Ancient India*, rpt., New Delhi, 1975.

Arora, U. P. : *Motifs in Indian Mythology*, New Delhi, 1981

Aryan, Subhashni : *Himadri Temples*, Shimla, 1954

Bandyopadhyay, B. : *Survey of Indian- Metal Sculpture*, New Delhi, 1987

Banerjea, J.N. : *Development of Hindu Iconography*, Calcutta, 1956

: *Religion in Art and Archaeology* (Vaishnavism and Saivism) Lucknow, 1968

Berreman, D. Gerrald : *Hindus of Himalayas*, Bombay, 1963.

Basham, A.L. : *The wonder that was India*, London, 1954

Bhattacharya, B.C. : *Indian Images-the Brahmanic Iconography*, New Delhi, rpt. 1978

Bhular, George : *Indian Palaeography*, trans. by J.F. Fleet(ed), Indian Antiquity, vol.XXXIII, 1904

Bhushan, Jamila Brij : *Indian Jewellery, Ornaments and Decorative Designs (2nd ed.)*, Bombay, 1964

Birdwood, G.C. M. : *The Arts of India*, New Delhi, 1997

Brown, Percy : *Indian Architecture (Buddhist and Hindu)*, Bombay, 3rd.ed., 1956

Chandra, Rai Govind : *Indian Symbolism*, Delhi, 1996

Chandra, Pramodh : *Studies in Indian Temple Architecture*, 1975

Charak, S.S. : *History and Culture of Himalayan States*, Delhi, 1978-79

Chauhan, Jaya : *Pabbar, Ittihas aivam Sanskriti*, Delhi, 2002

Claytn, A. C. : *The Rig-Veda and Vedic Religion*, rpt. New Delhi, 1981

Codrington, K. de B. : *Ancient India*, London, 1926

Coomaraswamy, A.K. : *Yaksha*, New Delhi, 1971

: *The Arts and Crafts of India and Ceylon*, London, 1913

: *The Dance of Shiva*, New York, 1957

: *Early Indian Architecture-Palaces*, New Delhi, 1975

Crooke, William : *Religion and Folklore of Northern India*, London, 1926

Cunningham, A. : *Coins of Ancient India*, London, 1891

: *The Ancient Geography of India*, rpt. Varanasi, 1970

: *Archaeological Survey of India:* Report XIV, 1978-79

Dasgupta, K.K. : *A Tribal History of Ancient India*, Calcutta, 1974

Deva, Krishna : *Temples of Northern India*, New Delhi, 1969.

Fabri, Charles : *An Introduction to Indian Architecture*, Bombay, 1963.

: *Discovering Indian Sculptures*, New Delhi, 1970

Fausball, V.S. : *Indian Mythology*, New Delhi, 1987

Fergusson, James : *History of Indian and Eastern Architecture*, vol.I , rept. New Delhi, 1987

Franke, A.H. : *Antiquities of India and Tibet*, Calcutta, 1914

Fraser, James Baillie : *The Himala Mountain*, Delhi, rpt.1982

Fredrick, W. Bunce : *An Encyclopaedia of Hindu Deties, Demi Gods, Godlings, Demons and Heroes*, 3 vol., New Delhi, 2000

Gatty, A. : *Ganesha* (2nd ed.), New Delhi, 1971

Gazetteers of the

: *Shimla District*, 1889-90, Delhi, rpt.,1992

: *Shimla Hill States*, 1910, Delhi, rpt., 1995

: *Sirmaur, Shimla,* 1969

: *British Garhwal*, 1910, rpt., New Delhi, 1994

Gerierson, George A. : *A Linguistic Survey of India*, vol. IX part IV, Calcutta,1916

Gupta, P.L. : Numismatic History of Himachal Pradesh, New Delhi, 1988

Goetz, Hermann : *Studies in the History of Kashmir and Western Himalayas*, Wiesbaden, 1969

: *Art and Architecture of Bikaner*, Oxford, 1950

: *Rajput Art and Architecture*, Wiesbaden, 1978

: *The Early Wooden Temples of Chamba*, Leiden, 1955

Harcourt, A.F.P. : *Himalyan District of Kooloo, Lahul & Spiti*, New Delhi, reprint 1972

Handa, O.C. : *Pahari Folk Art*, Bombay, 1975

: *Textiles, Costumes and Ornaments of the Western Himalayas*, Delhi, 1998

: *Temple Architecture of Western Himalaya, wooden temples*, New Delhi, 2001

Havell, E. B. : *The Himalayas in Indian Art*, London, 1924.

: *Encyclopaedia of Architecture in the Indian Subcontinent*, New Delhi, reprint 2004

Hopkins, E. Washburn : *Epic Mythology*, Delhi, rpt., 1974

Houson : *Epic Mythology*, Banaras, 1974

Iyer, K.B. : *Indian Art*: a short introduction, Bombay, 1958

Jain, Madhu : *The Abode of Mahashiva*, New Delhi, 1995

Joshi, M.P. : *Pragitihasik Madhya Himalya*, Almora, 1989

Kane P.V. : *History of Dharamshastra* Vol. IX, Poona

Khanduri, B.M. : *Archaeology of Alaknanda Valley*, New Delhi, 1994

Kramrisch, Stella : *Indian Sculpture*, Calcutta, 1933

Kramrisch, Stella : *Hindu Temples*, 2 vol., Delhi (rpt.), 1976.

Krishna, Brajesh : *The Art Under Gurjara-Pratihara*, New Delhi, 1989

Krishnan, Usha R. Bala : *Dance of the Peacock-Jewellery Tradition of India*, Kumar Meera Sushil Bombay, 1999

Law, Bimla Churan. : *Tribes in Ancient India*, Poona, 1943

Mackey, E. : *Early Indus civilization*

Mani, V.R. : The Cult of Weapons- *The Iconography of Ayudha Purusas*, New Delhi, 1985

Martin, E.O. : *The Gods of India*, Delhi, 1972

Mehta, Rustam : *The Handicrafts and Industrial Arts of India*, Bombay, 1960

Malhans, B.S. : 'Craftsmanship of Rohru-Chirgaon', Paper presented on a seminar on the History, Art and Archaeology of Himachal in Shimla. April, 1998 (unpublished)

Mian, Goverdhan Singh : *Art and Architecture of Himachal Pradesh*, Delhi, 1996

: *Festival, Fairs and Custom of Himachal Pradesh*, Delhi, 1992

Mishra, Indumati : *Pratima Vigyan*, Bhopal, 1979

Munday, G.C. : *Pen and Pencil sketches, being the journal of a tour in India*, 2 vol., London, 1832

Nagar, Shanti Lal : *Mahishasurmardini in Indian Art*, New Delhi, 2001

: *The Temples of Himachal Pradesh*, New Delhi, 1990

Ohri, V.C. : *Sculpture of Western Himalayas*, New Delhi, 1991

: ed. *History and Culture of Chamba State*, Delhi, 1988

: ed. *Art of Himachal, Shimla*, 1975

: ed. *Himachal Art and Archaeology: Some Aspects*, Shimla, 1980.

Pal, K. : *Crafts and Craftsmen in Traditional India*, New Delhi, 1978

Pallis, Marco : *Peaks and Lamas*, London, 1939.

Pandit, Vishshwar Reu : *Bharat ke Prachin Rajvansha*, 3vol., Jaipur, rpt. 2002

Pandey, L.P. : *Sun worship in Ancient India*, Delhi, 1971

Pargiter, F.E. : *Ancient Indian Historical Tradition*

Pawar, B.S. : *Uttrakhand Sangrahlya Darshan*, New Dehi, 2007

Piggot, Stuart : *Pre historic India, Penguin*, 1952

Postel, M. & Naven, A. : *Antiquities of Himachal Pradesh*, Bombay, 1985

Puri, Brij Nath : *The History of the Gurjara-Pratiharas*, Bombay, 1957

Rankin, Reginald. : *Tours in the Himalayas and beyond*, London, 1930.

Rao, T.A.G. : *Elements of Hindu Iconography*, 2 vol. (4 parts), Varanasi, rpt. 1971

Rose, H.A. : A *Glossary of the Tribes Castes of the Punjab and the North West Frontier*, New Delhi, rpt. 1999

Rowland, Benjamin, : *The Art and Architecture of India (2nd ed.)*, Penguin Book, 1956

Sairam, T.V. : *Indian temple, forms and foundation*, Delhi, 1982

Sankalia, H.D. : *Prehistory of India*, New Delhi, 1977

Sankrityayan, Rahul : *Himalaya Parichya*, Allahabad, 1953

Saklani, Dinesh : *Ethnic communities of Himalayas*, New Delhi,

Shah, Umakant.P. : *Glimpses of Nepal Woodwork*, Clacutta, 1968

Shashtri, Ajay Mitra : *Ancient Indian Heritage-Varahmihira's India*, 2 vol., New Delhi, 1996

Sarswati, S.K. : *A Survey of Indian Sculpture*, New Delhi, 1965

Sethi, S.M. : *Catalogue of Stone Sculptures in the Museums of Himachal Pradesh*, Shimla, 2002

Sethi, S.M., Chauhan, Hari : *Fountain Stone Slabs of Chamba*, Jaipur, 2006

Settor, S. (ed.) : *Memorial Stones*, Dharwad, 1982

Sampurnanand : *Hindu Deva Parivara Ka Vikas*, Allahabad, 1964

Sharma, B.N. : *Harsha and His Times*, Varanasi, 1970

Sharma, K.P. & Sethi, S.M.: *Costumes and Ornaments of Chamba*, New Delhi, 1997

Sharma, Roop Kumar : *Sirmour Darpan*, Sirmour, 1970

Sharan, M.K. : *Tribal Coins-A Study*, New Delhi, 1972

Siddhantashastree, R. K. : *Wood Carvings of Gujarat*, vol. V., part VII-A (2) Census of India, 1961

Singh, Om Prakash : *Religion and Iconography on Early Indian Coins*, Varanasi, 1978

Singh, Seo Bahadur : *Brahmanical Icons of Northern India*, New Delhi, 1977

Smith, H Clifford. : *The Art of Jewellery (Ancient and Medieval Period),* Delhi, 2002

Sivaramamurti, C. : *Skt. Literature, Art and Mirrors of Indian Culture*, Delhi, 1942

: *Sources of History Illustrated by Literature*, New Delhi, 1979

Thakur, Laxman S. : *The Architectural Heritage of Himachal Pradesh*, New Delhi, 1996.

: ed. *Where Mortal and Mountain God Meet*, Shimla, 2002

Tod, James : *Annals and Antiquities of Rajasthan*, New Delhi, 1978

Trivedi, Sudhir Kuma : *Madhya Bharat ki Pratiharkalin Kala aivam Sthapatya*, Jaipur, 1994

Untracht, Oppi : *Traditional Jewellery of India*, London, 1997

Vaidya, K.L. : *The Cultural Heritage of the Himalayas*, New Delhi, 1977

Vashisth, Sudarshan : *Himalya Main Sanskriti*, Delhi, 2006

Vt, M.S. Agarwal, V.S. : 'A note on the sculptures from Lakhamandala' JUPHS, XVII, pt.1, pp.87-89

Vogel, J. Ph., Hutchison : *History of Punjab Hill States*, New Delhi, Reprint 2000

: *Chamba State Gazetteer*, 1904

Vogel, J. Ph. : *Antiquities of Chamba States*, ASI, 1911

Watt, Sir George : *Indian Art, Delhi*

Yadav, Nirmala : *Ganesha in Indian Art and Literature*, Jaipur, 2000

Zimmer, Heinrich : *Myths and symbolism in Indian Art and civilization*, New York, (4th rpt.) 1963

INDEX

I

J

K

O

P

R

U

V

W

Y

Pl.1. Brahmi script in depleted condition.

Pl.2. Copper plate, a treaty signed between Raja Pritipati Shah and Raja Udai Singh of Bushair State, Samvata. 28 Fagun,1923.

Pl.3 Miniature temple, Bachoonch.

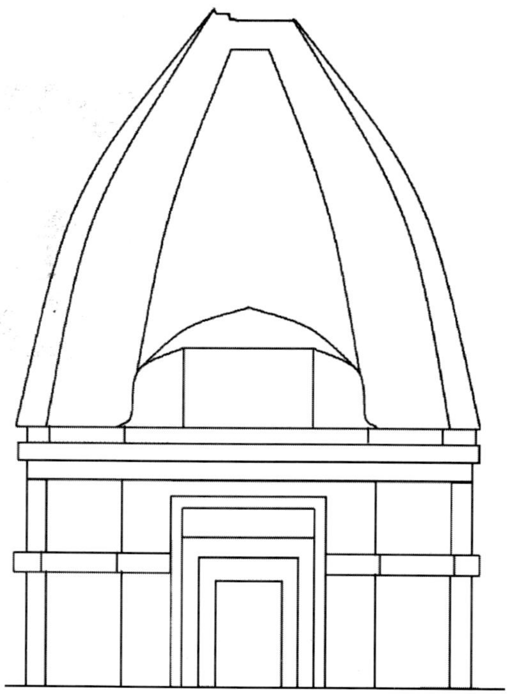

Pl.4 Shiva temple no.I, Parhat, front view.

Pl.5 Shiva temple No. II, Parhat.

Pl.6 Durga temple, Hatkoti.

Pl.7. Shiva temple, Hatkoti.

Pl.8 Shiva temple, Sawra.

Pl. 9. Symbols of local deities under open sky.

Pl. 10. Chaunra, symbols of deity placed under roof.

Pl. 11. Mahasu devta temple, Badiar.

Pl.12. Kainlu Devta temple, Rohtan.

Pl.13. Banar devta temple, Pujarli.

Pl.14. Shiva, Bachoonch, 10th century A.D.

Pl.15 Sthanakamurt Vishnu, Bachoonch, 10th century.

Pl. 16. Vishnumaunvartin,
Hatkoti c. 7th century.

Fig17. Garudasin Lakshmi-narayan,
Hatkoti, 10th cent.

Pl.18 Surya, Bachoonch, 10th cent. A.D.

Pl.19. Simavahini Durga, 8th cent. A.D.

Pl.20. Parvati, Bachoonch, 10th cent.A.D.

Pl.21 Mahishasurmardini, Bachoonch,10th cent. A.D.

Pl.22. Mahishasurmardini, Bachoonch, 9th cent.

Pl.23.Mahishasurmardini, Bachoonch, 8th cent.

Pl.24. Mahishasurmardini, Bachoonch,17th cent.

Pl.25. Mahishasurmardini, Bachoonch,17th cent.

Pl.26. Ganesha, Hatkoti, 9th cent. A.D.

Pl. 27. Ganesha, Bachoonch, 10th cent. A.D.

Pl.28. Ganesha, Bachoonch, 12th cent.A.D.

Pl.29. Ganesha, Hatkoti, 10th cent. A.D.

Pl.30. Pandva Sculptures, c.15th -16th century A D.

Pl.31. Mahishasuramardini (metal) Durga temple, Hatkoti.

Pl.32. Hero Stone, Hatkoti, 18th cent.

Pl.33. Sati Stone, Hatkoti
17th -18th cent.A.D.

Pl.34. Shant festival ceremony.

Pl.35. Jailly sliding on rope during Bhunda festival.

Pl.36. People dancing with blazing faggot in Jagra festival.

Pl.37.woodcarving Mahishasurmardini, Shiva temple, Hatkoti, 17th cent.

Pl.38.woodcarving Vishnu, Shiva temple, Hatkoti, 17th cent.

Pl.40. Three dimensional sculpture.

Pl.39. Woodcarving Durga temple, Hatkoti, 20th century.

Pl.41. Vishnu riding on Garuda, 17th cent. A.D.

Pl.42 (a). Bell metal dies having different motifs.

(b)

Pl.43. Women folk loaded with traditional silver jewellery.

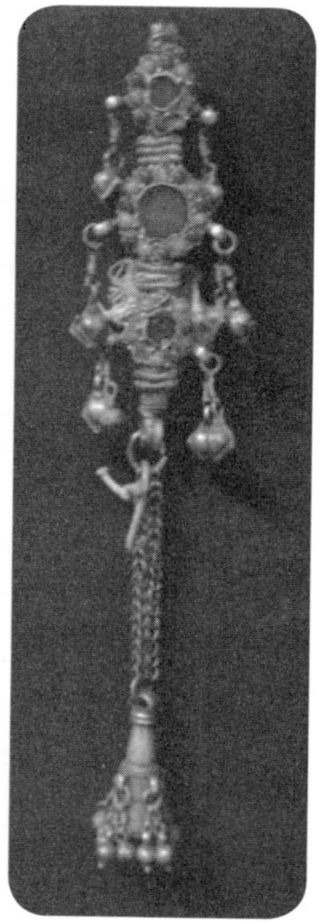

Pl. 44. Head ornament Jutti.

Pl.45. Ornament for forehead shingarpati, silver.

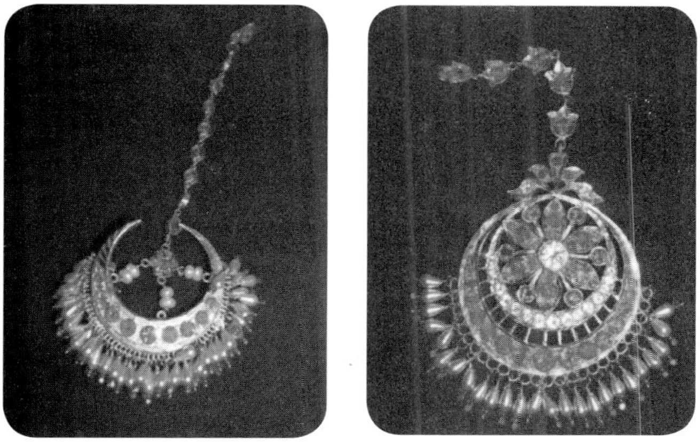

Pl.46. Mangtikka, gold.

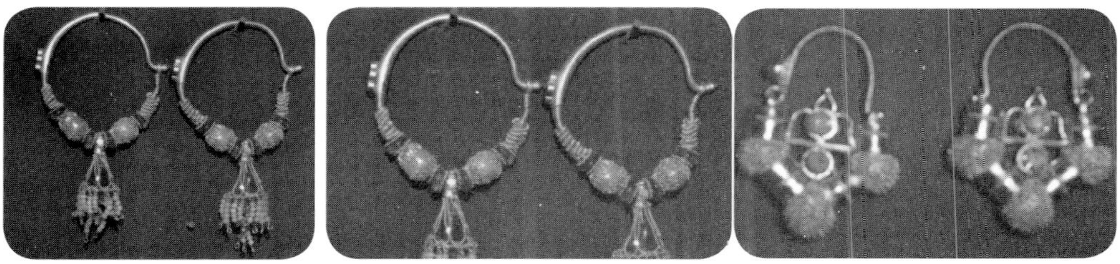

Pl.47.a,b,c. Ear ornaments, gold.

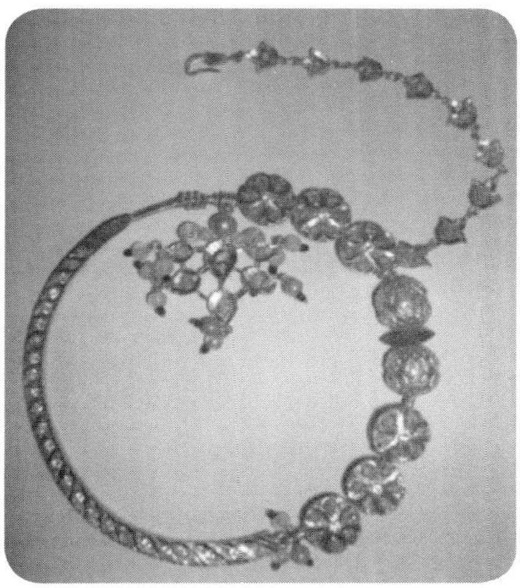

Pl.48.Balu-nose ornament, gold.

Pl.49. Chandrahar, silver.

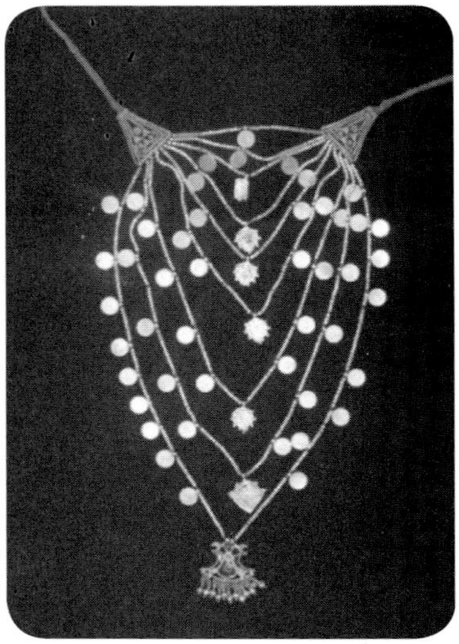

Pl.50. Hamel. neck ornament, silver.

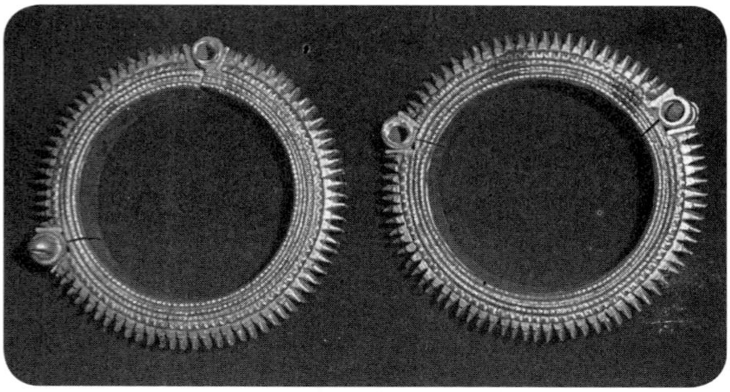

Pl. 51. Gajroo, wrist ornament, silver

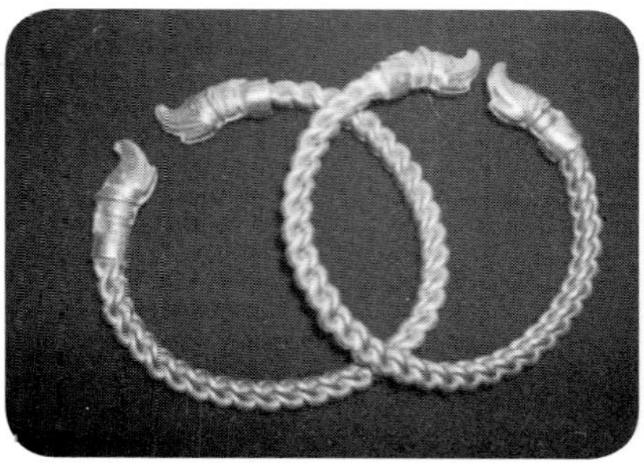

Pl. 52.(a) Sunangan, gold.

Pl.52. (b) dhagle, silver.